DECISIONS AT
15/16+

Also by Michael Smith and Veronica Matthew

Decisions at 13/14+
Decisions at 17/18+

DECISIONS AT 15/16+

Michael Smith

Headmaster, Filton High School, Bristol,
County of Avon

Veronica Matthew

Senior Lecturer, School of Law,
De Montfort University

CRAC

HOBSONS

Published by Hobsons Publishing PLC

CRAC

The Careers Research and Advisory Centre (CRAC) is a registered educational charity. Hobsons Publishing PLC produces CRAC publications under exclusive licence and royalty agreements.

ISBN: 1 85324 671 9

First published 1972 by the Careers Research and Advisory Centre. Reprinted 1991, 1992 and 1993.

Ref: L082/5t/H/JC

Printed and bound in Great Britain by JB Offset Ltd, Marks Tey, Colchester.
Cover illustration by Amanda Hall

CONTENTS

1. Where are you now? 4
2. Making the grade 12
3. People at work 41
4. The shape of things to come 63
5. You choose – more education and work later? 77
6. You choose – training now and work later? 107
7. Getting that job 131
8. What can you do with your qualifications? 145
9. Where can you find out more? 174

3

Where are you now?

Take a look at school life so far. Each year has been different. In year one everything was new, exciting and unexplored. By year two, you knew your way around. Year three was different – there were important course-choice decisions to be made, and year four saw a new opportunity to put them into practice.

Now it's year five and you have arrived. Top dog. The final year of schooling as far as the law is concerned. How does it look from where you stand now?

Freedom?
Choice?
Independence?
Time to do what you want?
End of homework?
No one on your back?

Probably nothing of the kind.

Look at a typical week in the fifth year. Sandy's diary gives you the evidence:

Monday	History homework due in 4.00pm Games practice Learn French 6.30pm Badminton
Tuesday	French test 10.30am Careers interview (remind Mum & Dad) 6.30pm Baby-sitting at the Bristowes (good nosh) Take Chemistry books. Do Maths homework.
Wednesday	My tutor group taking Assembly (read poem) Tuck shop duty at break 4.00pm Music lesson Geography and Biology coursework
Thursday	Timed essay in History Buzby wants to see me about Biology French and English homework Get ready for Maths test (again)
Friday	Geography project due in (Can I get an extension?) Get details of work experience (Can I choose the Merchant Navy?) English essay
Saturday	Early turn at shop 8.00am–12.00 Jill's birthday Orienteering at 2.00pm (not sure if I'm going) Disco at Capones
Sunday	Mock exams Lie in to 10.00 History, Maths, French homework

Most fifth-year students would probably claim that they have to put up with more this year than ever before.

There are a few well-known problems lurking here.

Let's give them an airing.

Many of them are so familiar that everyone's heard them before but that does not mean that everyone deals with them in exactly the same way.

You

If you have problems with your parents, you won't be the first. Spreading your wings and becoming independent is rarely painless. Probably they still see you as a child. Understandably you wish to be treated as an adult. Independence, however, is a process, not an event. To achieve it, it has to be worked at. Seeing others' points of view is a good starting point for both sides.

Relationships

Relationships with other people are never the easiest things to manage. They grow on confidence and experience – commodities which are at present in short supply. Some fifth-years feel isolated and underconfident, acutely aware of being too tall, too short, too fat, too thin or possessing some physical flaw which blots out all the other qualities in a quite illogical way. But every friendship made and continued even over a short period is a victory. Build on your successes and your relationships will grow in kind and depth of satisfaction.

Do you ever feel that school is hemming you in?

Many schools will progressively allow fifth-years more freedom than in previous years. Of course you feel different. You want recognition, status and individuality now. Believe it or not, this is just what school wants to give you, but it may not be able to go all the way all at once. Aggression is not the answer. Avoiding head-on collisions can work miracles. No school enjoys hassles with anyone, but a good school will always take issue with anyone who takes it for a ride.

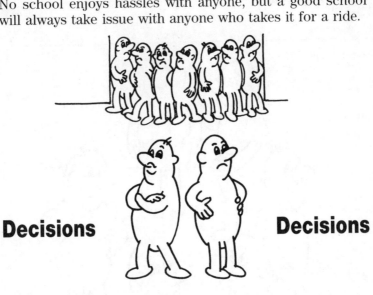

Decisions   Decisions

No matter what anyone says, decision-making is not easy. Decisions cannot be made to order, within a given time or under particular conditions. Neither, however, do they fall off a tree. They have to be worked at too. They flourish with an input of up-to-date, relevant facts. Starve them of these and they wither. They have a habit of growing in discussions with other people and, above all, need time to come right.

The fifth-year who enjoys every piece of set homework every night hasn't been born. The reality of the situation is that examination hurdles need practice if you are going to leap over them with ease. Look at it this way: if homework or coursework was fishing, soccer, drama, disco dancing (or whatever your particular thing is) you wouldn't complain. It is a matter of seeing what is worthwhile, commiting yourself to it and spending time on it.

Inevitably, hurdles loom. But get them in perspective. They are not the north face of the Eiger mountain – an almost insurmountable obstacle only fit for geniuses to tackle. If you have taken work seriously through the year you should obtain reasonable results. Exams are only a way of measuring how far you have succeeded and as such are nothing to be frightened of. They are designed to test what you know, understand and can do, not what you don't.

Important advice

Any of these issues can get out of proportion. If they, or any other problem, are being bothersome, talk them over with someone sympathetic. There is always help and advice about – usually more than you think.

Making the grade

Does your whole future depend on next summer's exams? Many fifth-years think so, but that is only part of the story. There is more to getting and holding a job than gaining grades in GCSE.

Do you need convincing?

Have these situations ever happened to you?

- How many times have you got cross with a shop assistant who has given you poor service?
- Would you like to be treated by a doctor who snaps your head off every time you go to the surgery?
- Have you ever been annoyed by a DJ at a disco who always plays out-of-date records?
- Did you regret going down to the market to buy that watch which has already packed in?
- Have you ever nearly been mown down on a zebra crossing by a lorry driver in a hurry who did not want to stop?
- Have you ever been kept waiting in an office while the secretaries occupied themselves making coffee?
- Did you enjoy waiting 40 minutes at the bus stop for the bus which eventually came late?
- Is it worth going to the cinema if the staff always rudely challenge you about your age?

What has caused these problems?

This is not to suggest that all secretaries are lazy, that doctors don't care, that lorry drivers are inconsiderate, that dealers are dishonest, or DJs incompetent. But these things can and do happen. Every time these situations do occur, they remind us that there is more to doing a job than being qualified for it. Attitudes are very important.

So qualifications do not matter?

Try another set of questions and decide for yourself.

So qualifications are unimportant?

- Would you agree to your tooth being extracted by a friend who was not a qualified dentist?

- Would you take your sick pet to an amateur veterinary surgeon?

- Your record-player, which was broken, has been mended by an unqualified electrician. It works now but is electrically unsafe. Would you use it?

- Would you like to travel to an overseas holiday centre flown by a pilot on his first day in the air?

Job ingredient missing

These questions are designed to help you understand what is meant by making the grade in the working sense.

It's QSAs that count	
Qualifications	Q
Skills	S
Attitudes	A

Check these situations and see what **qualifications**, **skills** or **attitudes** were missing.

Qualifications, skills and attitudes (QSAs) at work

MARY . . . . INFANT TEACHER

Mary spent four years following an education course at a polytechnic for her BEd (Hons) (**Q**) and is teaching (**S**) a reception class in an infant school where 27 very young children need her undivided attention (**A**) most of the day.

WAYNE . . . . LORRY DRIVER

Wayne qualified for his heavy-goods vehicle licence (**Q**) and obtained a job driving a tanker and delivering petrol (**S**) in the Home Counties. This means frequently negotiating busy and congested towns full of other drivers (**A**) for much of the week.

JENNIFER . . . . DENTIST

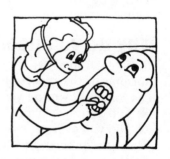

Jennifer went to university after A-levels to read dentistry. She obtained a BDS degree (**Q**). She then joined a practice in London caring for patients' teeth (**S**). The practice is growing in popularity because the local people appreciate the care which is shown (**A**) over their problems.

STEPHEN .... MAIL-ORDER CLERK

Stephen left school at 16+ to go to a college of further education where he passed his secretarial examinations (**Q**). He found employment with a mail-order company where he processes orders (**S**) given by demanding customers by letter and over the phone (**A**).

Everyone needs QSAs to work. Let's look at each one individually.

Agreed, school qualifications are not everything. They won't enable you to be a brain surgeon straight away. But they are an important first stage and they won't arrive automatically at the end of year five when the exam results come out. They have to be worked for and tackled systematically. And that means a sensible plan for revision . . .

Why do you need a plan?

Revision properly done will ensure confidence on the first morning of the mocks. Remember other examinations you have taken down the years:

● Did you ever panic the night before?
● Did you ever get flustered on the day and write rubbish?
● Were you cross with yourself for losing marks?
● Have you missed any vital stages of the work?

The only way to deal with these problems is to **plan** your revision.

Why have mock examinations?

In very few subjects, your GCSE may consist only of course work, but most will include formal exams. For some people, this is the first big formal test, at length, that they have ever experienced in a subject. You need to feel what it is like to sit in silence for up to two hours separated in all directions by one to two metres from your friends and be required to present work skills you have learned over the past two years. It is a necessary experience of the real thing and you should take it seriously.

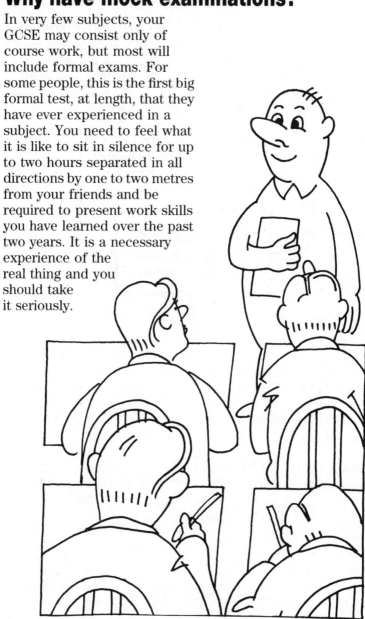

Countdown to the mock examinations

With your parents

Tell your parents your arrangements. Now is the time to negotiate time off from chores in return for study. Approach them in the right way and they will probably go out of their way to help you.

With your friends

Look at the commitments you have outside school – boyfriends/girlfriends/clubs and societies. Try to ensure they don't get in the way of work. Don't give up everything but strike a balance between work and leisure.

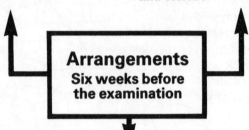

Arrangements
Six weeks before the examination

With yourself

Be realistic about revision. It is hard. It is boring. It is not rewarded immediately. There is no $^{10}/_{10}$ the next day. You have to cope with it together with your normal load.

Remember this is a trial run, so that if you get it wrong, there is a chance to put things right. Set up a checklist on a large sheet of paper and hang it in your room by your books.

Subjects to be taken	GCSE exam title and number	Exam board	Course-work required	Date deadlines

Sources

Arrange all your *books*, *folders* and *files* in order on a bookshelf where you can find them easily. Number books and pages. Index your files. Check with staff and friends to see you have the correct number. If there are any gaps, take steps to get what's missing. Obtain lost hand-outs. See that your mini-library is complete.

Planning

You then need to get down to planning your *subject* revision calendar. It will take a while to get into your stride, so run one subject into the next week to begin with. When choosing combinations of subjects, try to line up ones which demand different learning skills, so that you won't be bored, eg geography plus art, history plus music.

Subject revision calendar	
Week 1	Subjects A + B
Week 2	Subjects B + C
Week 3	Subjects C + D
Week 4	Subjects E + F
Week 5	Subjects G + H
Week 6	Your choice

Topics

You next need to identify *topics* within subjects. Sort out and organise the component parts of each subject so that you know what you are doing. You will then know precisely what you should be doing in each of the six revision weeks.

Suggested examples from

Biology

Systems of the body – digestive, nervous, etc
Plant functions
Cells
Ecology
Insects
Classification
Life histories, etc

Mathematics

Sets
Matrices
Scale drawings
Averages
Decimals
Volume
Angles
Graphs, etc

Methods

You must choose the one which serves you best. You could try:

Index cards

These are summaries of work neatly written on postcard-size cards to fit into your pocket for quick reminders. One approach that has been found useful is to pair with a friend and for each of you to prepare different sections which match each other.

Underlining

Go through your books and files underlining the key passages and essential points. Make sure your teacher approves of this method.

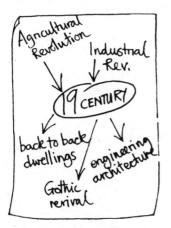

Flow diagrams

Pictures can be retained more easily than words. If they can describe a whole topic or illustrate a set of comparisons, they can be very helpful. They will also save time!

Trigger words

These are words which will trigger off your brain in the examination if they appear in the question. You can also use mnemonics for apparently unrelated lists of points.

eg
mnemonic for the
colours of the spectrum:
Robbers **O**f **Y**ork **G**o
Boating **I**n **V**enice

Short periods of real learning (not gazing out of the window!) followed by a shorter break concentrates your effort.

Self-testing is also important – on the same day and then in the same week, so that the material you have learned goes into your long-term memory. Little rewards can also be helpful.

When the examinations arrive:
● go to bed early the night before
● get together all the necessary equipment
● use the toilet before the exam starts
● get to the examination on time
● don't make idle comparisons of revision
● stay calm when the paper arrives
● watch your timing like a hawk.

After the results are published, take stock. This is a phase which should not be skimped as you will have learned valuable lessons about yourself.

After-the-exam checklist

1 How well prepared was I really for . . . ?
2 Is the mark received a fair measure of my work?
3 Where were the gaps in my knowledge?
4 Did I pace myself right in the exam?
5 Did I read the questions properly?
6 Did I do the right number in each section?
7 Did I have all the right equipment?
8 Were there sections of work I found I did not understand?
9 What are my priorities between now and next summer?
10 Compare performance in each subject.

Subject	What I should have got	Mock result

● Note the gaps.
● List what must be obtained.
● Ask your teacher for help if necessary.

On the big day

Advice to candidates

You have known they were coming for the last two years, so don't panic when they finally appear.

On the nights before the examinations, go to bed early. You will perform better if you are fresh. When you get up, eat a good breakfast.

Check your examination timetable for dates and times carefully. Missed examinations cannot be retaken in the same session.

Arrive at the examination room in good time. A flustered arrival may mean a disorganised paper.

Read the instructions two or three times, so that you know – really know – what the examiner wants you to do.

The examiners will assume you know only what you tell them.

Think and plan before you write.

Don't write an answer to a question that isn't there.

Don't be discouraged by the quantity of paper your neighbour may be using. He or she may be writing rubbish.

Make sure your planning leaves you enough time to answer the last questions properly.

When it's all over and you leave the examination room, don't hold a post-mortem. It is not worth it.

Best of luck!

When the real results come out in the summer you should be somewhere here:

GCSE	
Grade A	Equivalent to the former GCE O-level grades A to C and the former CSE grade 1
Grade B	
Grade C	
Grade D	Similar to GCE grade D or CSE grade 2
Grade E	Similar to GCE grade E or CSE grade 3
Grade F	Like CSE grade 4
Grade G	Like CSE grade 5

Ungraded	Ungraded in CSE & GCE

● Remember that this examination will have indicated what you can do more thoroughly than GCE or CSE used to do. These results will be based on more than just what your memory can produce in the exam room. The coursework, research and other assignments you tackled during the year will have been included.

● The grades you get will display the level of skill which you have shown you have developed. The teachers/trainers/employers who will be concerned with your next and later stages will be very interested in seeing just how good you are.

Qualifications are crucial. Do you want convincing?

A few years ago a survey was carried out with 8,000 representative fifth-years who left school in 1984. A summary of their destinations is shown below.

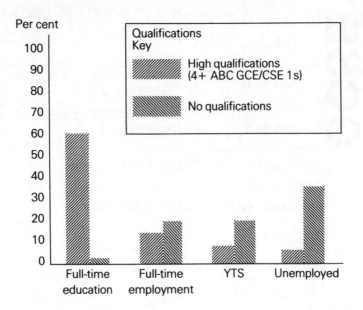

If the survey were taken today the figures would of course be different, since opportunities for employment have changed. It is not so much the proportion who went into the various categories that is important, but the comparisons, which make food for thought.

Look at who makes up each column by the qualifications they obtained before leaving school.

Where did those with no qualifications largely finish up?

What proportion of those with high qualifications got stuck on the dole?

The answers should be scary enough to make you double the time you spend on your homework straight away!

Qualifications may open doors to opportunities. Skills are needed to survive when you get there. They are many and varied, but broadly they are of two kinds.

● Social skills – skills needed to get on with other people.
● Life skills – personal competences used mainly with things and in activities.

To find some examples of what is meant, follow the flow chart below.

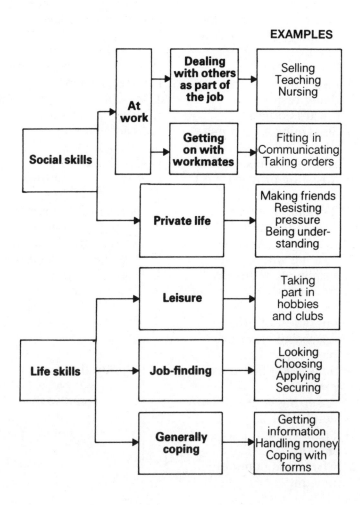

EXAMPLES

Social skills
- At work
  - Dealing with others as part of the job → Selling / Teaching / Nursing
  - Getting on with workmates → Fitting in / Communicating / Taking orders
- Private life → Making friends / Resisting pressure / Being understanding

Life skills
- Leisure → Taking part in hobbies and clubs
- Job-finding → Looking / Choosing / Applying / Securing
- Generally coping → Getting information / Handling money / Coping with forms

Here are some practical examples to show the difference between the two.

Social skills	Life Skills

Social skills	Life Skills
1 Communicating with others	A Formulating plans
2 Calculating your effect on others	B Making decisions
3 Controlling your temper	C Getting information
4 Resisting pressure from others	D Reading timetables
5 Persuading others	E Knowing the law
6 Listening to others	F Driving a vehicle
7 Being responsible towards others	G Handling money
8 Sustaining a conversation	H Finding accommodation
9 Making friends	I Getting a job
10 Resisting provocation	J Reading a 24-hour clock
11 Taking orders	K Using directories
12 Working in a team	L Reading a map
13 Taking the initiative	M Fitting a plug
14 Reading a situation	N Cooking a meal
15 Dealing with injustice	O Sewing on a button
16 Seeing an argument from another viewpoint	P Giving first-aid
17 Obtaining the co-operation of others	Q Estimating accounts
18 Assessing other people's capabilities	R Writing a report
19 Separating fact from prejudice	S Forecasting the weather
20 Asserting yourself with confidence	T Handling a keyboard
21 Speaking at a public meeting	U Using a telephone
22 Chairing a committee meeting	V Interpreting plans

Are there other
skills you
would wish
to add to
either column?

Skills are best appreciated in action. Try them for size in the story below.

TOM'S EVENTFUL DAY

Try to sort out which social and life skills Tom needed. The figures and numbers in the right-hand margin refer to the lists on page 28.

Tom's bad day.

Tom had had a bad day. The morning had not begun well. *There was a row* **3** over breakfast when he had had an argument with his younger sister Mary. She had got on his nerves, pestering him *to drive* her **F** and her three friends to the disco that evening. He had lost his temper with her. The last time he helped out they had *kept* **10** *him waiting* three-quarters of an hour and spoiled his plans for the evening. Not again.

Then the post had come. Barrington Tweed and Co had written to say that *they could not offer him work* because he had *failed a telephone test* they had given him as part of his interview and they regarded this as an essential feature of the job for which he had applied. The morning dragged on. He spent half an hour *replacing a button on his shirt.* It was now noon.

I

U

O

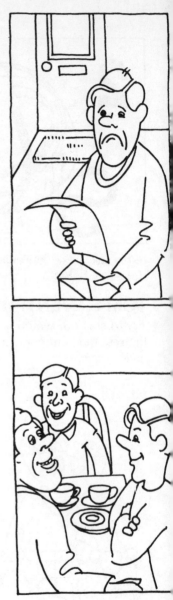

There was a knock on the door. Shaun and Wayne called to take him to the Kingfisher for coffee and a doughnut. He could not really afford it *but he did not want to let his friends down.* They were good mates and they *usually enjoyed his jokes.* Sometimes they had *serious discussions* from which he always *learned something.* So he went.

4

9

8

6

Coming out of the cafe he pulled out his Post Office Savings book. Less there than he thought. Why only a credit total of £84.53? There was over £100 there last week. This week's dole was yet to be added but even so . . . Then he remembered. He had *bought* some new jeans last week when he *really did not* **G** *need them.* They were a bargain though.

Feeling miserable, Tom made his way home. Pausing in front of the gate, he looked down the street and *froze at what he* **14** *saw.* A small boy – he could hardly have been four – was disappearing underneath a parked articulated lorry. Without noticing the lad, the driver had climbed up into his cab, slammed the door and started the engine. *Without further* **7** *thought,* Tom ran the 50 metres to the front of the lorry and *waved his arms* **13** *furiously* as the driver was revving up to leave. He was not pleased at being stopped and was not **10** slow *to tell Tom what he thought of his antics.*

Tom calmed him down and pointed beneath the lorry. Between them they dragged from underneath the rear wheels a grimy four year-old clutching a ball. Apart from oil stains and a couple of grazes where he had scraped the exhaust, he was unharmed. Tom and the driver looked around. There was no one about who appeared to own him.

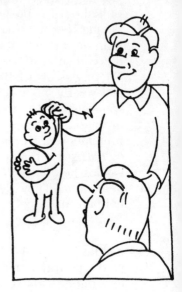

C Then they *noticed a piece of card* sticking out of his pocket. On the card were the words JOHNSON, Dentist, 14.30. It was a possible clue. Tom went over to the phone box and

K *went through the Js* in the directory looking for dental surgeons. He found two. The receptionist at the first was distinctly acidic when he asked whether a patient owning a four year-old child had an appointment at 2.30. *She told him to mind his own*

15 *business* and hung up. Instead of ringing her back to tell her what he thought, he tried a second time, *explaining more*

1 *carefully* what he was about. The plan worked.

The little boy's mother was there and was horrified to hear what had happened. She said she had left him playing with a friend who was going to take him to

7 the dentist. *She asked* Tom to look after Stephen, the four year-old, and bring him to her home in Petersham Close. He had

L to *check the street map* before he could be sure where to take Stephen but, as they walked together through the streets, Tom wondered whether he was

U *quite the telephone nitwit* that Barrington Tweed and Co had considered him.

A whole range of social and life skills are at work here. Some you will take for granted; others need working on to make them effective. Unlike qualifications, which are there or not as the case may be, social and life skills cannot be so easily measured. There are no universally recognised yardsticks of success. What will be acceptable in one situation will be inadequate in another. One's own performance varies from day to day as well, depending on many external circumstances. Nevertheless you can identify many of the most important skills and check your probable responses.

3 ATTITUDES

Of the three QSA ingredients, this is both the most difficult to pin down and the hardest to put right if there is something wrong. Our attitudes go to the root of our personalities. Coming out a new person tomorrow morning is not as easy as taking a bath.

They spring from our view of other people, who may not be folk we warm to straight away.

> *'Get out of my way; can't you see*
> *I'm in a hurry.'*
> *'Who does she think she is?'*
> *'He's only been here a week; now he is*
> *throwing his weight about.'*
> *'She couldn't ever smile back.'*
> *'If he thinks I am going to work with him,*
> *he had better think again.'*
> *'I'm never going to speak to her again.'*

Solutions to these sour grapes (and there are solutions) are beyond the scope of this book, but they serve to remind us that attitudes can be summed up by whether we like or dislike other people.

Look at the scene beyond school. There are a whole range of people with whom to get on:

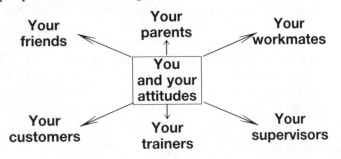

Attitudes are the parts of your personality which cannot be hidden. Every day at work will produce situations which make them public.

Are you willing to learn new things?

Everyone likes being secure. If you are being successful in a routine job well within your skills, this can be very satisfying. It will not last for ever. Moving on will mean going beyond the familiar boundaries of what you know you can cope with. New demands can bring insecurity if you don't prepare yourself to deal with them. There are training opportunities which will prevent your feeling threatened. Whether or not you take them will depend on you.

Are you prepared to make allowances for difficult workmates?

Unless you propose to be a hermit and write your bestseller in splendid isolation, every job will bring with it a collection of workmates. How you get on with them is crucial. They will not be perfect. They will have their own peculiar ways. They will expect you to fit in and may resent the

new recruit. How you handle this will be crucial to your job satisfaction. The way you get on with others at school will give you some idea whether you have problems ahead.

Are you prepared to go beyond what is asked for?

These days most occupations have job descriptions, so it should be clear what is expected of you. There are no rules, however, which prevent you going the extra mile, putting on an additional polish or going out of your way to be helpful. The company which takes more care is the one which is likely to attract more business. And that's your future assured.

Are you willing to accept responsibility?

Being part of a business means taking a share of some level of responsibility. How you react to this is certain to affect a whole range of activities undertaken by many others. If you have the skill, extra responsibility can be welcome in terms of job satisfaction.

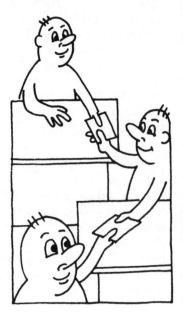

Do you accept unpleasant tasks willingly?

Life is rarely one great social whirl. Every job has its boring bits. You are going to have to decide whether to skimp the distasteful parts or to accept them willingly. Your boss will be very interested to see how you cope – whether you take them in your stride or moan endlessly. Your ultimate promotion could depend on your attitude to the dull and repetitive parts of your work.

Do you recognise your own weaknesses?

Nobody's perfect, but if you pretend to other people that you are, it will land you in trouble. When you have made a mistake, be open about it to the most appropriate person. Admitting your error before it is discovered by the boss is a positive approach which people in business appreciate. If you have done something for which criticism is justified, the skill of accepting it willingly, without going into a sulk, is worth cultivating.

Attitude problems are often self-centred. The difficulty is that they depend more on the way *we* see things than on objective events.

Take Joe and his boss, for instance. They each make statements about the same situation. Unless they sort themselves out, there's trouble looming.

Joe says:		Joe's boss says:
'I'm stuck in this job. No one pays any attention to me. I'll never get anywhere.'	**WHICH ONE IS RIGHT?**	'He never shows any real interest or enthusiasm for his work, so I don't think I will promote him.'
'I'm bored with my job. It's dull and I want to be moved to more interesting work.'	**WHICH ONE IS RIGHT?**	'He wants to push ahead too fast. He hasn't even mastered the skills of his present job.'
'He always tells me the bad things I've done. He never says anything about the good things.'	**WHICH ONE IS RIGHT?**	'He drives me crazy, making the same mistakes over and over again. Does he ever do anything right?'
'He's so fussy when I come in a few minutes late in the morning, even when I'm willing to stay later in the afternoon.'	**WHICH ONE IS RIGHT?**	'He doesn't know the meaning of punctuality. He thinks he can be late whenever he wants to and make it up at the end of the day when he's not needed.'
'I've been on the same machine for a year now. It's high time they put me on to something else.'	**WHICH ONE IS RIGHT?**	'He's only been here a year and wants to go on to something else – just when he's getting useful to me.'

The last word on QSAs comes from an employer

International Electronics Limited

Dear student,

I'm grateful for the opportunity to write this letter because we employers need help to find staff of the right calibre, just as you need help to find suitable jobs.

My high-technology company has been actively recruiting for a variety of non-manual positions for over 12 months. Out of the hundreds of applicants only a handful have measured up to our needs, and the majority didn't even have the fundamental attributes required. What are these?

Firstly, a candidate must be literate and numerate. What chance is there of selling our products if customers receive quotations which are ambiguously worded, misspelt and have the prices incorrectly added up? How can our production and quality control departments manufacture acceptable products if development departments provide them with drawings incorrectly dimensioned and with incomprehensible assembly instructions? In a technical job, the relevant technical educational qualification is also needed, together with a logical approach to problem-solving, which such a course should provide. For example, to design a new circuit it is essential to know and understand the characteristics of a wide variety of standard components and circuit designs, and to be able to combine these in a novel way to produce, at least in theory, the desired result.

Our second basic requirement is that the candidate should have the appropriate basic skills for the job. Skill development is related to practical experience,

International Electronics Limited

and the level of skill attainment we look for depends on the level at which we are recruiting. For example, we would expect a junior engineer designing a circuit to have the practical knowledge and skill to select the optimum components and wield a soldering iron. He/she can turn the circuit designed on paper into a piece of hardware which actually does what it is supposed to! So skills are all about converting knowledge learned from books into a practically useful output which, one way or another, can be sold to pay the wages.

Our final yardstick against which we measure candidates is in many ways the most critical, since it's the most obvious in any selection procedure; it's his/her personal presentation and attitudes. The scruffy, inarticulate, lacklustre candidate won't even get a hearing. We expect an effort to be made at the interview. We want to see interest in the job and the determination to succeed. We expect the candidate to show enthusiasm for work, career and life in general. Only then are we likely to get a conscientious, hard-working employee who'll pay his/her way. Conversely, we have employed staff deficient in both education and skills, simply because of their enthusiasm and innate potential and our consequent confidence that they will therefore 'make the grade'.

To summarise, if you're looking for a successful and satisfying career, gain all the educational qualifications you can, develop your practical skills, present yourself well and for heaven's sake show enthusiasm for your chosen career. If you aren't prepared to make the effort, please don't come knocking on my door.

Yours sincerely,

J Scarborough

J Scarborough

People at work

A world of work in layers

During the last 50 years, the world of work has undergone considerable changes. A great deal of specialisation has taken place on account of ever-increasing technological development, which requires a whole variety of special skills. Take the record industry, for example.

Getting the discs the public will buy

What you want	What this means	Skills needed
Quality recording	Freedom from background noise and interference; well-balanced, realistic sound.	Expert engineering skills in studio planning*1 and equipment design*2. Competent recording techniques*3.
Reasonable price	A retail price which covers costs, makes a profit for the performer and manufacturer, and provides the best quality without putting it beyond your pocket.	Effective planning and cost coverage*4. Ability to make records within these limits*5. Factory organisation*6 and maintenance*7. Industrial and personal relations*8.
Availability	Appearance in the shops at the time you want it – not running out of stock before most people who want it have had a chance to buy it.	Effective storage*9 and packing*10. Organised distribution, delivery*11 and sales*12. Accurate book-keeping and sensible customer relations*13.

*See who is responsible by consulting the cast list on page 43.

Each skill mentioned can be represented by a well-known career. The list is not exhaustive. There are other careers involved in record production, but these will do as a start.

The first listing helps you to identify the relevant careers, while the second sorts them into groups which can readily be compared.

CAST IN ORDER OF APPEARANCE
* **1** Architect
* **2** Recording engineer
* **3** Maintenance technician
* **4** Accountant
* **5** Process operative
* **6** Production unit manager
* **7** Maintenance engineer
* **8** Personnel officer
* **9** Storekeeper
* **10** Packer
* **11** Driver
* **12** Salesperson
* **13** Retail manager

CAST ARRANGED IN CAREER GROUPS

* **1** Architect * **2** Recording engineer * **4** Accountant * **8** Personnel officer	**Group A**	Highly trained people with professional qualifications. They try to solve new problems with new methods. They guide, direct and control the enterprise.	TECHNOLOGISTS
* **3** Maintenance technician *13 Retail manager * **6** Production unit manager	**Group B**	Very skilled persons who work closely with Group A. They interpret their decisions and accept specialist responsibilities for their part of the process.	TECHNICIANS
*11 Driver * **7** Maintenance engineer *12 Salesperson	**Group C**	Particularly skilled, practical people whose contribution is largely made by their hands.	SKILLED
* **5** Process operative *10 Packer * **9** Storekeeper	**Group D**	Important people in a more limited field. Their contribution may be of a more routine nature and their degree of skill will be varied.	OPERATIVES

These four groups can be found in most industries and the labels given to the groups can be applied to many business concerns. They form a useful framework within which to explore careers.

Group A Technologist **Group B Technician**
Group C Skilled   **Group D Operative**

Who makes cheese?

Technologist
Professional cheese-maker who is responsible for the entire process within the manufacturing plant. Directs research and development of new products.

Technician
Responsible for the daily, practical cheese process, he or she works manually within prescribed guidelines – exercising skill in a stage-by-stage process.

Skilled
Responsible for detailed product-testing at all stages of the process, making scientific investigations to ensure the maintenance of quality.

Operative
Responsible for routine, essential stages in process; reception of milk, weighing, checking, cleansing and stacking of churns. Packing and despatch of cheese.

Who makes trains?

Technologist
Professional engineers who have developed the concept of the high-speed train – thinking through the whole project from idea to reality.

Technician
Skilled engineers who provide detail designs, data and information to assist in the detailed development of the project.

Skilled
Practical engineers who use their skill to make parts and assemble them. The quality and effectiveness of the finished product is their responsibility.

Operative
Supporting workers whose co-operation on the more routine aspects of production is essential to its success.

This framework can be applied to people providing services. Suppose you are unwell and you visit your doctor. You are put in hospital until you are fit again. Track the careers involved and fit them into a similar grid.

Your problem	Medical person	Group

You are ill with an unspecified disease. You are taken into hospital. On arrival you will be shown to a ward which you will expect to be clean, and taken to a bed which has been made up with clean linen.

Nursing auxiliary — **Operative**

Your temperature, pulse and other data will be taken by a nurse who may also bring you your food if and when you are feeling hungry. Directing visitors, keeping them at bay, controlling the conditions of your life and recovery will be their chief concern. No one will provide a magic cure for your complaint.

Qualified nurse* — **Skilled**

What is wrong with you may be revealed by a series of blood tests which need microscopic examination. Your samples will be whisked away to a section of the hospital you will never see, and carefully investigated by a medical laboratory technician.

Medical laboratory scientific officer — **Technician**

* Title and qualifications will vary according to the locality.

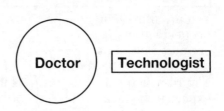

| **Your problem** | **Medical person** | **Group** |

Without the information thus provided, the doctor, whose responsibility it is to decide what is wrong with you and to direct your treatment, will find it exceptionally difficult, and in some cases impossible, to take a professional decision. Armed with the facts, he or she is able to decide how to treat you, what drugs should be administered, how much and how often, and will remain in control of these decisions until you are well.

This illustration is, of course, only a simplified example. Some nurses (especially Registered General Nurses) undertake such specialist functions that they belong more aptly to the technician bracket.

You can see at a glance how all these levels connect with one another to produce a single end product – your despatch from hospital as a recovered patient. It is a waste of time to say that only one level is important. Poor service in any one can wreck the work of the other three. Good work in all four will improve the quality of the whole process.

You can find examples of this framework in very many career fields. When you make comparisons between the different areas of the world of work, these layers begin to emerge. The table overleaf illustrates the point.

	Engin-eering	Business	Building	Retailing
Oper-ative	Metal machinist	Filing clerk	Site labourer	Store-keeper
Skilled	Instrument maker	Typist	Joiner	Floor manager
Tech-nician	Draughts-person	Office manager	Contracts manager	Buyer
Tech-nologist	Develop-ment engineer	Chartered accountant	Architect	Company secretary

Search
Draw up a table to illustrate these levels for other career fields.

Oper-ative				
Skilled				
Tech-nician				
Tech-nologist				

Looking at the layers

Although the levels shown here are part of a whole, there are two things which keep them apart.

Before you find a job in the level of your choice you will need training. This may mean a training course, a course in a college of further education or higher education to equip you with the skills you need. Training can be found either on the job, by release from work or on full-time courses.

Choose the training you need for the level of employment you want.

The training you start on will depend to some extent on the school qualifications you gain. Examination results are the keys which open training doors. Check the school exams you need to start the training course of your choice.

There are always dangers with over-simplification but, broadly speaking, the components of age, qualifications, courses and levels of employment add up to this:

Age	School qualifications	Training	Level of work
16+ 17+	Internal school examinations and reports and/or some GCSEs, grades D to G Pre-vocational course	Training courses, on-the-job courses or industrial training and some evening classes	Operative
16+ 17+	Up to 3 GCSEs, grades A to C, with others between D to F CGLI foundation courses Pre-vocational course	Training courses: some college day release, possibly block-release courses and some full-time courses	Skilled
16/ 17	4+ GCSEs, grades A to C CGLI foundation courses and further study	Training courses where appropriate. Some full-time further education vocational courses and some block-release	Technician
18+	2+ GCE A-levels, grades A to E AS-levels BTEC national	Full-time courses in institutions of higher education like polytechnics and universities	Technologist

NB: Course requirements may vary between colleges.

One of the risks of failing to see the wood for the trees is to assume that the routes are simple parallel tracks. In fact there are many complicated crossover junctions which increase your opportunities. Below is a diagram of the routes which are open.

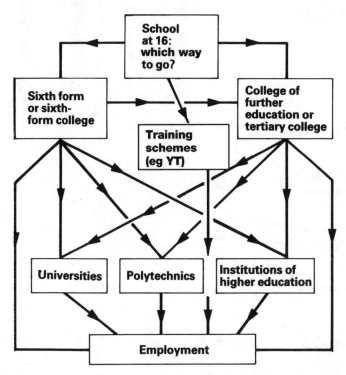

Everyone starts at the top box and hopefully will finish at the bottom. The important question is, *Which route will you take to get there?*

Careers and the layers in which they are available

We now need to be more detailed and to examine the idea set out above in terms of particular careers. The careers groupings overleaf will probably be familiar, and these have been labelled A to H for convenience. The levels down the side are numbered 1 to 4 and it is therefore easy to place on the grid any career you may wish to consider.

Families of careers		OPERATIVE 1	SKILLED 2	TECHNICIAN 3	TECHNOLOGIST 4
Scientific	A				
Social service	B				
Persuading/ influencing	C				
Literary	D				
Artistic	E				
Computational	F				
Practical	G				
Active/ outdoor	H				

Here are some ideas of careers listed in their family groupings and followed by grid references.

Choose a career family and check out its members

Scientific

Agriculture A1/2/3/4
Air traffic control A3/4
Animal technician work A2
Archaeology A4
Architectural technician
    work A3
Architecture A4
Astronomy A4
Audiology technician
    work A2

Baking technology A3/4
Biochemistry A4
Biology A3/4
Botany A4
Brewing technology A3/4
Broadcasting A2/3/4
Building control A3
Building surveying A3/4

Camera work (film & TV)
    A2/3/4
Cardiological technician
    work A2/3
Ceramics technology A3/4
Cartography A2/3/4
Chemistry A3/4
Chiropody A3/4
Computer programming
    A3/4

Computer systems
    analyst A3/4

Darkroom technician
    work A1/2
Data-processing
    management A3/4
Dental hygiene work A3
Dental surgery assistant
    A2/3
Dental technician work
    A2/3
Dentistry A4
Dietetics A3/4
Dispensing (optics) A3
Dispensing (pharmacy) A2
District nursing A2/3/4
Dry-cleaning A1/2/3

Engineering (all branches – chartered, technician engineer, technician) A3/4
Environmental health A4

Factory inspection A4
Film production A2/3/4
Forestry A1/2/3/4
Foundry technology A3/4
Fuel science A3/4

Geology A4

Health visiting A3/4
Home economics A1/2/3/4
Horticulture A1/2/3/4

Information science A4

Laboratory technician work A2/3/4
Leather technology A2/3/4
Librarianship A4

Medical laboratory scientific work A3/4
Medical photography A3/4
Medical physics technician work A3/4
Medicine A4
Metallurgy A3/4
Meteorology A3/4
Midwifery A2/3/4
Mine surveying A4
Museum work A4

Neurophysiology technician work A2/3
Nursing A2/3/4

Nutrition A3/4

Occupational therapy A3/4
Operational research A4
Ophthalmic optics A4
Ordnance survey work A2/3
Orthoptics A4
Osteopathy A4

Paint technology A2/3/4
Patent work A4
Pharmacy A4
Photography A3/4
Physics A3/4
Physiotherapy A4
Piloting aircraft A3/4
Plastics technology A3/4
Poultry husbandry A1/2/3/4
Printing technology A3/4
Psychology A4

Radiography A3
Rubber technology A3/4

Speech therapy A4
Surgery A4
Surveying A4

Town and country planning A4
Trading standards administration A4

Veterinary nursing A2
Veterinary work A4

Zookeeping A1/2/3/4

If that did not suit, try another one

Social service

Air cabin crew B1/2/3

Careers work B4
Chiropody B3/4
Church work B1/2/3/4
Consumer advice work B3

Dental hygiene work B3
Dental surgery assistant B2/3
Dentistry B4
Dispensing (optics) B3
Dispensing (pharmacy) B2
District nursing B2/3/4

Factory inspection B4
Fire service B1/2

Health visiting B3/4
Hotel reception B2/3
Housing management B4

Justices' clerk's work B4

Librarianship B4

Medical records work B2/3
Medical secretarial work B2/3
Medicine B4
Midwifery B2/3/4
Museum work B4

Nursery nursing B2
Nursing B2/3/4

Occupational therapy B3/4
Orthoptics B4
Osteopathy B4

Personnel management B3/4
Physiotherapy B4
Police work B2/3/4
Prison service B1/4
Probation work B4
Psychology B4

Radiography B3
Reception B1/2

Security work B1/2
Solicitor's work B4
Social work B4
Speech therapy B4
Surgery B4

Telephonist B1/2
Town and country planning B4
Trading standards administration B4

Youth work B3/4

Persuading/influencing

Acting C1/2/3/4
Advertising C3/4
Antique dealing C1/2/3/4
Auctioneering C3/4

The Bar (barrister) C4

Church work C1/2/3/4
Copywriting C3/4
Courier C2/3

Estate agency C3/4
Exporting C3/4

Grocery C1/2

Home service advising C3/4
Hotel management C3/4

Insurance C3/4
Ironmongery C1/2

Jewellery (retail) C1/2
Journalism C3/4

Land management C4

Marketing C3/4

Nursery nursing C2
Nursing C2/3/4

Occupational therapy C3/4
Organisation and methods C2/3/4
Orthoptics C4
Osteopathy C4

Personnel management C3/4
Physiotherapy C4
Police work C2/3/4
Prison service C1/4
Probation work C4
Public relations C3/4

Recreation management C3/4
Retail management C3/4

Shop work C1/2
Solicitor's work C4
Speech therapy C4
Stockbroking C3

Teaching C3/4
Travel agency work C2/3

Literary

Acting D1/2/3/4
Archive work D4

Broadcasting D2/3/4

Copywriting D3/4

Film production
D2/3/4

Interpreting D2/3/4

Journalism D3

Public relations D3/4

Stage management D2/3/4

Translating D2/3/4
TV and stage production
D2/3/4

Artistic

Antique dealing E1/2/3/4
Archaeology E4
Architectural technician
work E3
Architecture E4
Art E1/2/3/4

Ballet E1/2/3/4
Beauty therapy E2/3

Camera work (film & TV)
E2/3/4
Cartography E2/3/4
Ceramics design E2/3/4

Choreography E1/2/3/4
Commercial art E1/2/3/4
Compositing E2

Dancing E1/2/3/4
Display work E3
Dressmaking E1/2/3

Embroidery E1/2
Exhibition design E3/4

Fashion buying E2/3/4
Fashion design E2/3/4
Film production E2/3/4
Floristry E1/2

Furniture design E2/3/4

Goldsmithing E1/2
Graphic design E2/3/4
Graphic reproduction E2/3

Hairdressing E1/2

Interior design E2/3/4

Jewellery E2/3/4

Landscape architecture E4
Layout artist E2/3/4

Millinery production E1/2
Modelling and sculpture
    E3/4
Modelling (fashion) E1/2
Musical performance
    E1/2/3

Photography E3/4
Pottery E1/2/3/4
Print finishing and binding
    E2
Print machine operating E2

Sculpture E3/4
Set design E2/3/4
Silversmithing E1/2
Signwriting E1/2

Tailoring E1/2
Textile design E2/3/4
Town and country planning
    E4
Typography E2/3/4

Upholstery E1/2

Wardrobe mistress' work
    E1/2/3

Computational

Accountancy F3/4
Accountancy technician
    work F3
Actuarial work F4
Air traffic control F3/4
Architectural technician
    work F3
Architecture F4
Astronomy F4

Banking F3/4
Building society work F3/4
Building surveying F3/4
Buying F2/3/4

Cashier's work F1/2

Company secretary's work
    F3/4
Computer operation F3
Computer programming
    F3/4
Computer systems analyst
    F3/4
Cost accountancy F3/4

Data processing F3/4

Economics F4
Engineering (chartered,
    technician engineer,
    technician–all branches)
    F3/4

Insurance F3/4

Market research F4
Mathematics F3/4
Meteorology F3/4

Organisation and methods F2/3/4

Physics F3/4

Purchasing F3/4

Quantity surveying F2/3/4

Statistics F2/3/4
Stockbroking F3
Surveying F4

Work study F2/3/4

Practical

Ambulance work G1/2
Animal technician work G2
Assembly work G1

Baking process work G1
Beekeeping G3
Binding G1/2
Blacksmithing G1/2
Brewing process work G1
Bricklaying G1/2
Builders' labourer G1
Bus driving G1
Butchery G1/2

Cabinet-making G1/2
Canal work G1
Canning process work G1
Carpentry G1/2
Catering assistance work G1/2
Ceramics craft G1/2
Chef's work G1/2/3
Chiropody G3/4
Cinema attendant's work G1
Coastguard work G1/2

Confectionery preparation G1/2
Cookery G1/2/3
Crane driving G1

Dental hygiene work G3
Dental surgery assistant G2/3
Dentistry G4
Docks and harbour work G1/2
Domestic work G1
Dressmaking G1/2/3
Dry-cleaning G1/2/3

Embroidery G1/2

Engineering (craft and operator level–all branches) G1/2

Farming G1/2/3/4
Farriery G1/2
Film projection G1/2
Fire service G1/2
Fishing G1/2
Fitting G1/2
Floristry G1/2
Forestry G1/3/4

Gamekeeping G1/2
Game warden work G1/2
Gardening G1/2/3/4
Gas fitting G1/2
Glazing G1/2
Goldsmithing G1/2
Groundsman's work G1/2

Hairdressing G1/2
Home economics G1/2/3/4
Horses, work with G1/2/3
Horticulture G1/2/3/4
Hosiery work G1/2
Hotel work G1/2

Ironmongery G1/2

Jewellery G1/2/3/4
Joinery G1/2

Kennel work G1

Laboratory technician work G2/3/4
Laundry work G1/2/3

Massage G1/2/3
Mechanic's work G1/2
Merchant navy G2/3
Midwifery G2/3/4
Milkroundsman's work G1
Milk process work G1
Millinery production G1/2
Milling (engineering) G1/2
Mining G1/2
Motor mechanic's work G1/2

Nature conservancy G1/2/4
Nursery nursing G2
Nursing G2/3/4

Occupational therapy G3/4
Ophthalmic optics G4
Ordnance survey work G2/3
Orthoptics G4
Osteopathy G4

More practical

Packing G1
Painting and decorating
  G1/2
Panel beating G1/2
Park and garden
  maintenance G1/2/3/4
Patrol work AA/RAC G1/2
Pattern-making G1/2
Physiotherapy G4
Piano manufacturing and
  tuning G1/2
Piloting aircraft G3/4
Pipefitting G1/2
Plastering G1/2
Plumbing G1/2
Postal delivery work G1
Pottery craft G1/2
Poultry husbandry G1/2/3/4
Print finishing G2
Print machine operating G2
Professional sport G1

Quarrying G1/2

Radio and TV repairing G1/2
Refuse collecting G1
Roofing G1/2

Sawmilling G1/2
Sewing machinist's work
  G1/2
Sheet metal work G1/2
Shepherd's/shepherdess'
  work G1/2/3
Shop work G1/2
Signalman's work G1/2
Signwriting G1/2

Silversmithing G1/2
Slating G1/2
Spray painting G1
Stable work G1
Stock control G1/2/3
Stonemason's work G1/2
Surgery G4

Tailoring G1/2
Tanning G1/2
Taxi driving G1
Theatre attendant's work
  G1
Tiling G1/2
Tool-making G1/2
Traffic warden's work G1
Trawler fishing G1/2
Typing G1/2/3

Upholstery G1/2

Veterinary nursing G2
Veterinary work G4

Waiting G1
Wardrobe mistress' work
  G1/2/3
Watch and clock repairing
  G1/2
Welding G1/2
Woodworking (machinist)
  G1
Zookeeping G1/2/3/4

Active/ourdoor

Agriculture H1/2/3/4
Armed services H1/2/3/4

Beekeeping H3
Bricklaying H1/2
Builders' labourer H1

Canal work H1
Carpentry H1/2
Coastguard work H1/2
Courier's work H2/3
Crane driving H1

Diving H1/2
Docks and harbour work
   H1/2
Driving H1

Farming H1/2/3/4
Farriery H1/2
Fire service H1/2
Fishing H1/2
Forestry H1/3/4

Gamekeeping H1/2
Game warden's work H1/2
Gardening H1/2/3/4
Glazing H1/2
Groundsman's work H1/2

Horses, work with H1/2/3
Horticulture H1/2/3/4

Jockey's work H1

Kennel work H1
Landscape architecture H4

Lorry driving H2

Merchant navy H2/3
Milkroundsman's work H1

Nature conservancy H1/2/4

Ordnance survey work H2/3

Painting and decorating
   H1/2
Park and garden
   maintenance H1/2/3/4
Patrol work AA/RAC H1/2
Piloting aircraft H3/4
Poultry husbandry H1/2/3/4
Professional sport H1

Quarrying H1/2

Refuse collection H1
Roofing H1/2

Shepherd's/shepherdess'
   work H1/2/3
Signwriting H1/2
Slating H1/2
Stable work H1

Taxi driving H1
Tiling H1/2
Traffic warden's work H1
Trawler fishing H1/2

Veterinary nursing H2
Veterinary work H4

Zookeeping H1/2/3/4

The shape of
things to come

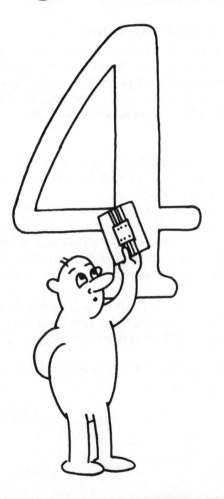

The good old days

Without manufacturing industries, life as we know it would come to a full stop. For the last 200 years, they have had a central place in the life of the country, by:

● providing goods people want
● giving employment to a workforce
● putting money in people's pockets
● creating wealth (through taxes) to provide services (hospitals, roads, etc).

Problems rock the boat

There is a certain rhythm to raw materials being turned into finished products by a series of well-tried processes which keeps a good number of people in employment in a wide range of occupations. Over the past decade, that pattern has seen a series of interruptions resulting from a number of challenges.

● There has been a great deal of competition from northern Europe, North America and Japan, especially in the area of high-tech consumer goods.
● People tend to be paid less in southern Europe and in the countries of the Pacific. Goods from these countries, therefore, cost less to make. This makes such imports attractive to the customer in the High Street compared to similar but more expensive products made in the UK.

Despite the boom of the late 1980s, unemployment has risen again as the world recession hit British industry in the early 90s. By August 1992 unemployment stood at 2.75 million.

The cartoons opposite tell the story from the point of view of one imaginary company.

An expanding economy

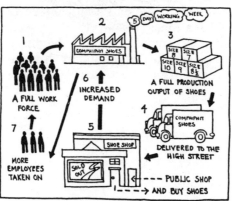

A contracting economy

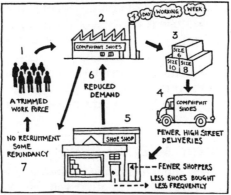

This is, of course, telling the story very simply. It is not just a matter of buying an extra pair of shoes to create more jobs and put the economy straight. There are a whole host of factors which have an effect on employment – wages, cost of raw materials, overseas competition and government policy. Through all the complexities, however, the message is clear. If the production cycle slows down, everyone suffers:

At points

1 Some people will lose their jobs. No school-leavers are taken on.
2 The factory is a tenser place to work in.
4 Fewer deliveries will be needed.
5 Shops employ fewer assistants.
7 Management have some tough decisions to take.

Enter the magic chip

Alongside these economic and political changes there have been technological ones. Discovery never stands still. Scientists have been busy exploiting the possibilities of slivers of silicon only a few millimetres square, on which electronic circuits are printed, carrying information very efficiently.

They are:
- tiny
- reliable
- fast
- flexible
- cheap to make
- getting more sophisticated yearly.

As powerful as a roomful of computers of several years ago, this small powerhouse is capable of receiving, selecting and communicating information so quickly that it can out-think the human brain in some functions (though it possesses no creativity and is without emotions). There is hardly any aspect of manufacturing and supporting services to which it has not been applied. There are massive changes on the job front too.

All aboard for science fiction

These chips are in the information technology business (IT for short). This means that, whether you are collecting data for weather forecasting from clouds two miles up or instructing a machine to drill a three millimetre hole, the chip is gathering, storing, retrieving and passing on information which results in something being done. You can put it to work in a thousand different ways and this has been happening since the 1980s. Silicon chips (micro-electronics, to give them their sophisticated name) are used in:
- televised information (CEEFAX, ORACLE, PRESTEL)
- music synthesisers
- mail sorting
- robotic car assembly lines
- airline seat booking

- cash dispensing outside banks
- television games
- body scanners in hospitals
- computer-marked examinations
- electronic toys
- weather satellites
- electronic news gathering
- word processors
- home computers
- retail goods sales control
- petrol dispensing
- pocket calculators
- cordless telephones.

In Japan, there is even a factory where robots are making robots!

In every case, the arrival of the chip has meant a massive improvement in the process concerned.

Things to come

Information technology does not stand still. Looking into the future is never easy, but below are a few not too silly ideas which will probably become commonplace within the foreseeable future:

- being able to manage your bank account by pressing buttons on your television set
- having your car partly controlled on the motorway by signals automatically picked up from the road
- travelling on driverless trains
- dictating a letter into a machine which shows up on a screen in Australia without the aid of a secretary
- using the public reference library through an electronic connection to your home
- translating a book from a foreign language by computer
- talking to the USA by phone for nearly the same charge as a local call
- writing on an electronic blackboard and seeing the result displayed on a television screen
- having your illness diagnosed by computer
- doing business without money.

Your town today

INFORMATION TECHNOLOGY Effective diagnoses and treatment must be based on accurate information. Sophisticated equipment to analyse patients' conditions is only possible through a microcontrol system.

Hospital

INFORMATION TECHNOLOGY Those curious bars on the packet you buy in the supermarket are the evidence. They form part of a sophisticated stock ordering, distribution and finance control system.

Shopping precinct

Offices

INFORMATION TECHNOLOGY Offices deal essentially in information and the decisions resulting from it. Word processors, computer-stored data and computerised telephone/telex systems increase efficiency.

INFORMATION TECHNOLOGY
ORACLE/CEEFAX/PRESTEL provide instantaneous news. Video recorders extend leisure and home-education facilities. Home computers are now common. Special equipment for the handicapped is also being developed.

INFORMATION TECHNOLOGY
Local government needs facts and figures to plan its roads, schools, health clinics, libraries and a wide range of social services. Computers are essential tools if the correct decisions are to be made.

Housing

Town Hall

Factories

School

INFORMATION TECHNOLOGY
Adverts of cars being made by robotos are familiar. A wide range of goods is now being made partly by robots which are accurate, reliable and take a lot of the monotony out of work.

INFORMATION TECHNOLOGY
Computer studies are now commonplace in many secondary schools. School administration is now being assisted by microcomputers.

The Daily Telegraph, Saturday

MICROCHIP TO SPEED BUSES

By our Transport Correspondent

A £21 MILLION plan for the computer centre for London buses was unveiled yesterday.

Loops of cable buried in roads would activate radio links to show exactly where every bus was, with a central control room able to send instructions to drivers via a display panel in every cab.

A pilot scheme costing £1,700,000 is planned on three routes which run across the West End and out to Lewisham in the South East and in the opposite direction to the North West suburbs of routes 36, 36A and 36B.

Eventually the system could be extended so that a display panel at every bus stop would tell passengers of any delays and when the next bus would arrive.

£8m yearly savings

The system is designed to improve reliability, said London Transport. "It will be able to get information to and from as many as 15 buses a second."

Mr Martin Wheatley, in charge of the development team, said it was the tool that route controllers have been waiting for. It would enable problems to be spotted long before they became serious. "It brings the microprocessor into the working lives of bus crews."

London Transport expects it to bring savings of around £8 million a year, so the system would soon pay for itself.

Most London buses will be fitted with emergency radios by the end of this year. But lack of frequencies means that voice communication with a control centre is very limited. Normally it is reserved for emergencies such as an assault on the crew.

Reprinted with the permission of the *Daily Telegraph*.

More jobs or fewer?

There is no doubt about the usefulness of the microelectronic revolution. Just as the first industrial revolution transformed the lives of those living in the late 18th and early 19th centuries, when machines replaced muscles, information technology will take over some thought processes hitherto carried out by the brain. This could have a devastating effect on peoples' jobs. Some will totally disappear. New ones will emerge.

Some examples, not in any way an exhaustive list, are:

Fewer	More
Assembly hands	Computer programmers
Filing clerks	Systems analysts
Inspectors	Television manufacturers
Machinists	Electronic engineers
Proofreaders	Robot designers
Material handlers	Aerospace engineers
Book keepers	Installation operatives
Meter readers	Technicians of all kinds
Copy typists.	Geriatric care staff
	Leisure industry staff.

Two other points should be noted. The IT revolution will change jobs but not necessarily evenly or predictably across the board. Developments in auto engineering are likely to phase out some present workers (craft electricians) and invent others (exhaust emission control engineers). Driver navigation aids are likely to increase work on assembly lines and on motorways. It could also be argued that there will be fewer jobs if industry fails to keep up with the new technology. Competition from abroad will see to that.
If we get the revolution right and ensure that microelectronics boost production at competitive rates, then more wealth will be created to plough back into society.

This will improve leisure services, hospital care and assistance to the older generation (everyone is likely to be living longer by the turn of the century). If we use the chip in this way, it will mean more work (of a different kind) rather than less.

Changes in lifestyles will be inevitable. Small businesses should be able to flourish with cheap computing power at their elbow. We may see a massive growth of home-based employment. Transport will be less necessary for the masses, but where it exists it is likely to be better organised. Work sharing may become common; overtime may become a historical curiosity; earlier retirement may become the norm. Community service may become more widespread. Leisure activities will grow. But this is all guesswork. In the early days of the railway, pessimists predicted that all kinds of disasters would befall the human body if projected along a track at a speed in excess of 30 mph. Musicians who took a gloomy view of the first gramophone records got it all wrong.

One thing remains certain. The job challenges facing the 15+ generation are daunting and demanding.

Crystal ball gazing

There are several implications for you which arise from all this change. Take first the structure of employment, ie the increases and decreases in the national demand for different types of occupation. The diagram below shows what has been happening to date and projects these changes through to 1995. The base line 0 represents a no change situation. Everything above is an increase; below, a decrease.

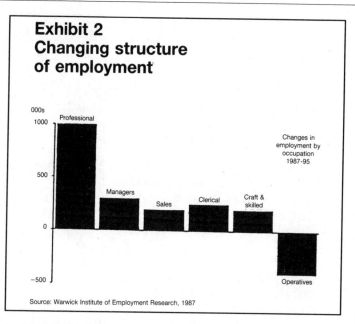

Exhibit 2 is taken from the CBI publication *Towards a Skills Revolution,* and is reproduced with their permission.

The message is clear. For those keen to get ahead, prepare yourselves for one of the growth areas.

There are other needs you should note. In spite of the changes (or perhaps because of them) certain skills are at a premium, ie whoever you are, whatever happens, wherever you are working, you will need to be particularly good at certain things if you are going to succeed.

Particular skills needed for the working world of the 1990s

☐ Skills in *applied technology* – not playing with computers for the sake of them, but using the state of the art to store and retrieve information, solve problems and apply solutions.

☐ Skills in *working in a European partnership* – using a modern European language with ease, being willing to work anywhere throughout the European Community.

☐ Skills in *understanding how the world of work operates* – making informed decisions, seeing the wood for the trees, understanding where your bit of the industrial enterprise fits in and what contribution it makes to business as a whole.

☐ Skills in *personal relations* – seeing the issue from the other person's standpoint and working co-operatively with others towards a mutually agreed objective. The ability to get on with others whose views differ from yours, without departing from the values you hold to be important.

☐ Skills in *communication* – the ability to set out ideas in words and pictures, eg writing reports or drawing up plans, with the important features highlighted. The facility to express yourself orally without getting tongue-tied.

☐ Skills in *numeracy* – the ability to use numerically-based information (including statistics, graphs, flow charts, spreadsheets and models). The skills of estimation, calculation and projection are important here.

NOW PUT YOURSELF TO THE TEST . . .

How good are you at using these necessary skills for the 1990s?	Probably very capable	Reasonably competent	Passable	Not particularly good	Would have to work hard at it
Using applied technology					
Working in a European partnership					
Understanding how the world of work operates					
Personal relationships					
Communications					
Numeracy					

Complete this self-assessment and then ask a friend to fill in their assessment of you. Are there any differences?

You choose – more education and work later?

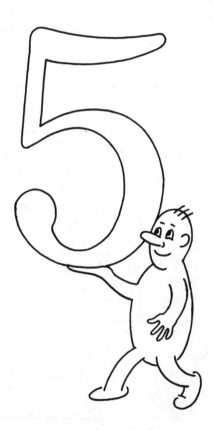

What, more examinations? Could be. In the first part of the book we have seen that, although 15+ is an important milestone, it is not necessarily the finishing post. There are very good reasons for this. Important as they are, GCSE qualifications are just not good enough for many careers. A higher level of entry is necessary – that could mean GCE A-level, taken at 17+.

It's not just that entrance qualifications are going up (although this has been the pattern over the past 20 years). The entrance demands of many careers have increased because of the complexity of the science and technology which lie behind them. A rapidly changing world of work needs a constant supply of highly trained, flexible specialists who are qualified in the arts, humanities or sciences. Take, for example, a high-tech industry producing silicon chips.

How we design and make silicon chips

A company which designs, develops and manufactures silicon chips needs people with an amazing variety of technical skills: chemists and physicists to develop and understand the basic raw materials connected with their design and development; electrical and electronic engineers to develop, operate and maintain complex and often very expensive production and test equipment; computer experts to develop, manage and operate advanced computer systems for design, test and production processes.

Silicon chip manufacture is carried out under extremely clean conditions where everyone is required to wear specialised clothing, the air is filtered, and entry is through airlocks to make sure that all activities are undertaken in as dust-free an atmosphere as possible. When working with dimensions measured in millionths of a metre the importance of this can be understood. The degree of accuracy required can only be achieved with the aid of computer-based design and layout techniques, and the circuits can only be tested reliably by using complex computer-aided equipment.

Finally, the chip must be mounted into a package suitable for insertion into a printed circuit board. Advanced computer-programmed assembly machines are used to achieve the delicate task of taking hundreds of incredibly fine gold wires from a chip less than ¼ inch square, and bonding them onto pads smaller than a pin head.

NB Pages 79-81 appear by courtesy of the Engineering Careers Information Service publication *New Dimensions in Engineering Careers*, available free from EITB Publications, PO Box 75, Stockport, Cheshire DK4 1PH.

This sheet was developed by:
ECIS and Marconi Electronic Devices Ltd, Lincoln.

Career opportunities

Building up confidence – RACHEL SARGENT

After passing my A-levels in maths, physics and chemistry, I obtained a place on a three-year degree course in electronic engineering.

As part of my degree course, I am doing a one-year project at Marconi's advanced semiconductor factory in Lincoln.

When I first entered Marconi, I was struck by the modern factory environment and perhaps more particularly by the informal and open atmosphere created by the engineers I was going to work with. I must say that this was different from the impression I had formed about the engineering environment at school, and was a very pleasant surprise.

So far I have worked alongside application engineers in the Integrated Circuit Department, where circuits are developed to meet the particular needs of a variety of industries – for example, chips which will work in push-button telephones and the new digital telephone exchanges. The work involves logic design, and much of it is carried out with the aid of advanced computer graphics workstations and associated test equipment. This is very expensive, but I soon learned to use it as a matter of course, which has built up my personal confidence a lot.

Making the theory work – DEREK YOUNGSON

I have a degree in physics and electronics and decided that I wanted to get involved specifically in the manufacture of silicon chips. I also wanted to work for a company which would give me access to a broad range of technologies.

I was aware that my formal education at school and college had given little, if any, insight into manufacturing techniques and processes, and was delighted when I learned that Marconi were prepared to give me training in practical manufacturing skills. When my application was accepted, I started work in the wafer fabrication clean rooms.

I found that I could quickly relate the theory I had learned, to the jobs in hand and start to play a positive role in operating the incredibly expensive computer-controlled equipment which is essential for the production of silicon wafers.

The job is very demanding, requiring self-confidence and personal motivation together with an ability to work for long periods under pressure in a very precise and controlled environment.

There is great demand for people with these particular skills and I am confident that I am on a secure career path.

Developing the software – MALCOLM SMITH

I am a sponsored student and am doing a year's work experience before I go to university.

My particular interest is in writing software programs and I want to make use of this in my career.

I have already been given the opportunity to get involved in computer-based electronics in a wide range of technologies, many of them at the raw edge.

The equipment I am using is the most advanced available and I am being trained to make software work in practical situations rather than just to produce games and special computer effects.

I find that in general I am very much left to solve problems in my own way, but if I need help, it is readily forthcoming and the objectives of my projects are very clearly defined.

I am basically practically-minded and the workshop training connected with my Engineering Software Project is tending to make me think that my career aspirations are leading to electronic sub-systems design.

Would you fit into a world like this? It's a hard question to answer. Your difficulty lies in looking ahead five years or more and knowing for sure:
● where you ought to be
● what you can cope with
● how successful you could be
● what opportunities there will be.
This is where advice, trust and commitment come in.
The magic formula is:

Advice from teachers to go ahead with A-levels		Backing from parents for two years' study		Worth starting on a GCE A-level course		Your own willingness to work hard at it
	+		+		=	

If any of these three counters is missing, you should think about other routes from 16+. If they are all present, seize the opportunity, for, without doubt, your careers opportunities will improve.

What is A-level like?

Just as GCSE was taken in separate subjects, GCE A-level is also a single-subject exam. There is a great deal of difference, however, in the number of subjects taken:
● most people take three subjects
● a few sit four
● taking two is very worthwhile indeed
● sitting one is limiting but far from useless, especially with a good range of GCSEs behind you.

Taking one, two or three subjects sounds very specialised, and it could be if you allow it. There is no limit on the combinations of subjects you can take (but you need to check with your careers adviser because some combinations are more useful than others). One way to avoid over-specialisation is to consider AS-levels (see overleaf.)

Some people find the work at A-level much more demanding than at GCSE. In some subjects there is a greater emphasis placed on writing essays than previously and it is only fair to point out that it is a more difficult course than that running up to 16. Certainly it is more theoretically based. Many people would argue that there is a greater gap to leap between GCSE and A-level than A-level and undergraduate studies at university. If you have five or six GCSE grades A to C in a good breadth of subjects, however, you should be able to cope.

Keeping you balanced through to 18

There has been a recent development to broaden sixth-form courses by the introduction of AS-level (AS = Advanced Supplementary). These are sixth-form courses in half A-level units and, as such, the normal three A-levels student could consider two A-level subjects plus two AS-levels instead. This would allow the curriculum to be broader, since four areas would be your focus of attention, and you could avoid excessive specialisation.

Whether a school or college makes them available is a matter of choice, usually decided by resources. Universities have generally welcomed AS-levels from candidates seeking entrance, accepting two AS-level subjects instead of a third A-level. There is, however, no question of requiring or even preferring them, so your university chances will not be reduced if you cannot sit them.

Some misconceptions have spread regarding AS-levels and you should be aware of them. AS-levels are:

● NOT of a lower standard of difficulty than A-levels
● NOT necessarily one-year courses
● NOT a half-way stepping stone to A-level
● NOT a bolt-on extra for the student already studying three or four A-levels.

They are meant to contrast with and complement your A-level courses, so keeping your options and possibilities as flexible as possible.

For more details on AS-levels and how particular universities regard them, consult *University Entrance – Going to University*, published by the Committee of Vice-Chancellors and Principals and the Standing Conference on University Entrance.

How do I choose my A-levels?

There are a number of points from which you start to answer a question like this. Take first the careers reference point. By the time you have completed the end of your fifth year you could be looking at sixth-form options from a vocational angle. At that time you will:

1 know your career intentions, or

2 have only a general career idea, or

3 accept that no career plan has yet emerged.

What steps should you take in each one of these cases?

1 If you know your career intentions

If you have made up your mind about a future career and confirmed this choice with your careers teacher, careers officer, subject teachers, parents and other interested people, then you will know what the entry requirements are in terms of examination passes and whether the career involves further education or on-the-job training. This will give you a target to aim at while you are at school, which might be GCE A-levels, AS-levels, GCSEs, or any combination of these. You will have a good idea after taking examinations in the fifth year, and discussing the results with staff at school, where your respective subject strengths and weaknesses lie – this should help you with your subject choice for the sixth form. So, if you can clearly see your career destination, find out the subject requirements for it and build a well-balanced programme around them.

2 If you have only a general career idea

Those of you who have broadly chosen your career field, but who are not certain exactly which career you would like to aim at, are in a more difficult position and must therefore get all the help and advice you can. This can come from your school's careers teachers, the careers officer, other staff and, of course, your parents. But remember, none of them are fortune-tellers; they can only give advice and information – *you* have to make the final choice.

Perhaps you will decide to leave the career decision open by looking at a broad group of careers – such as social services or engineering. If this is so, then you should aim at a particular level of entry, eg graduate, professional or technician. According to the structure of the career or again, with advice from the careers staff, you can pinpoint the subjects needed to reach this goal. If you have decided upon the 18+ entry, for example, you may discover that the career group you have chosen involves high ability in mathematics. Your subject teachers will soon tell you whether they think you might reach a satisfactory standard at A-level. You will then know whether your target is realistic. Likewise, for technician-level entry into your broad career group, you are likely to require a minimum of four GCSE grades A to C to commence training – you must find out whether this is within your grasp and, of course, in which subjects it is desirable or possible.

It's all a matter of balancing what you want against what they need.

3 If you have no career plan at all

Those of you who have no idea what career you would like to follow, should consider the subjects you enjoy doing and, usually related closely to this, those you are good at. If you have a broad base of GCSE grades at C or above and, for example, enjoy a science subject such as physics and have achieved a fair measure of success in it, then this would clearly be a natural choice for A-level.

As a full A-level programme usually involves following three subjects you should now consider which others would be the most appropriate to do with physics – they are likely to be scientific or mathematical subjects. This will keep as many doors open as possible, which is the best idea for anyone who has no definite career in mind. The other subjects might be either pure and applied mathematics, or pure mathematics on its own, chemistry and/or biology.

Alternatively you could look at subject choice from the **learning point of view**. Take study methods and implications as your reference point and ask yourself the following twelve questions:

1 What kind of skill does each subject demand?
2 How much factual learning will be involved?
3 Does the course involve a problem-solving approach?
4 Is there any overlap between the subject areas I am considering?
5 Do my subjects form a sensible pattern?
6 How important will any command of written English be?
7 Is wide reading necessary for success?
8 Is fifth-year success a good predictor in my case?
9 How appealing is a new subject never previously studied?
10 At sixth-form level, how important is the teacher element as a determining factor?
11 Will there be any practical work in the examination?
12 Are my basic interests well represented in the final choice of subjects?

For further reading consult
Your Choice of A-levels,
available from
CRAC/Hobsons Publishing PLC

Jobs and Careers after A-levels

A guide for people
who are looking for a job after A-levels
plus career profiles of 42 successful job-seekers
MARY MUNRO

CRAC

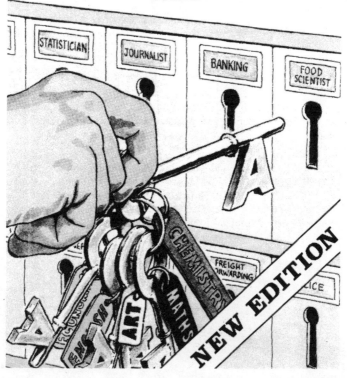

What form will the results take?

Achievement at GCE A-level is measured in letter grades, as with GCSE; A to E being regarded as A-level passes. Marks over 60% are graded B or A while the proportion of marks awarded to grades C, D and E are equalised. The bottom of grade E should be seen as just over 40% of the total possible marks. N spans the same number of marks below E as the D spans above E. Its principal value lies in recording a near miss, since it is a better result than ungraded and could help employers, advisers and candidates alike to work out appropriate courses of action. The distribution of marks overall looks like this:

Distribution of A-level grades

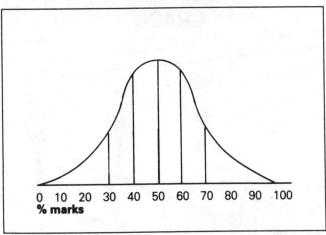

© School Curriculum Development Committee

90

Benefits from taking A-level

Apart from the results themselves, there are other benefits on offer at the end of the A-level course.

BENEFIT 1
Your career plans will change and develop as you grow older. By doing an A-level course you have built in a useful two-year delay before having to commit yourself.

BENEFIT 2
Having A-level passes gives you keys to open a wider range of careers doors. Check this out for yourself in chapter eight.

BENEFIT 3
You will have changed too. The vocational training you start at 18 is likely to be more of a success than if you had begun it earlier.

BENEFIT 4
Having A-levels to your credit often gives exemption from particular professional examinations.

BENEFIT 5
If you decide to go for employment at 18, you should interview better in competition with younger applicants. Extra maturity gives you greater confidence.

BENEFIT 6
Your A-levels could, in some cases, increase your salary over those who entered the same business at 16.

BENEFIT 7
The A-level route is the one most frequently used to take you to college, polytechnic or university.

Of course, no one can guarantee you either a higher education place or particular employment at the end of A-levels. Experience of those who went before you, however, suggests very strongly that your chances will be better.

But A-level may not be your scene. Has sixth-form education anything to offer for those interested in shorter courses?

One-year courses

There is no law which demands that your GCSE qualifications must be obtained at the end of your fifth year. Some people will have gained the odd subject in the fourth while others will need six years to collect a reasonable spread of good results. It could well be that you will take a range of subjects in the fifth and will want to extend them in the sixth. The exact subjects you study will depend on what your school has to offer. Your course could probably include a combination of these possibilities:

Regrading

Subjects which you took at GCSE but in which the grades you obtained were not as high as you would have liked, can be taken again. You should note, however, that winter retakes are on the way out.

New subjects

Subjects which are new to you may have a particular attraction. They will vary according to the curriculum of your school but examples of this category are geology, Greek civilisation, sociology and economics.

Old favourites

There may be some subjects you dropped when you made your course choices towards the end of the third year, because you could not fit them all into the pattern for years four and five. Examples of these could be music, home economics and religious education.

Vocational courses

Subjects are sometimes offered which fulfil certain specific career needs – commercial, engineering and pre-nursing courses. They are invaluable bridges between school and vocational training since they help you test out your interest in and suitability for that career, as well as preparing you for the training yet to come. The school subjects which comprise these areas are usually as follows:

Course	Core subjects studied	Career use
Business	Shorthand, typing, office practice, accounts, the business environment	Office clerk, shorthand typist, secretary
Pre-nursing	English, human biology, chemistry or balanced science, home economics	Nursing, nursery nursing, nursery and infant welfare assistant, etc
Engineering	Mathematics (including perhaps additional maths), physics or balanced science, craft, design and technology	Technician (mechanical, electrical or civil engineering), draughtsman, etc

Another feature of these courses is often a close liaison with local industry and/or a college of further education. This could mean that part of your course would be spent in a firm or at a college which specialises in a particular field. This can form an introduction to a career, from which you can progress to a course in a college of further education or continue training in employment. It would not yet be true to say that this kind of arrangement is common, but it is on the increase and, where it does operate, you can profit from a combination of related studies and work experience which will give you very valuable preparation for your future career. Such courses do not produce ready-trained secretaries, nurses or engineers, but they prepare the way admirably.

Vocational courses

There are a number of ways in which useful subjects can be put together to allow your basic education to be built on and extended through to 17+. The main areas of the curriculum, like English and mathematics, are usually represented. The humanities and creative subjects are often to be found but, at this level, increasingly vocationally useful subjects join them. Vocational courses are offered by City and Guilds, the RSA Examinations Board and BTEC. Their programmes are listed below.

City and Guilds Diploma of Vocational Education

Intermediate level
- can be studied alongside A-levels, or done singly in one year.
- a choice of nine vocational areas
- more than 100 modules within the areas, eg advertising, and building construction.

National level
- two-year programme with units of study similar to those above
- will be aligned to GNVQs when they are introduced.

In addition to the Diploma, successful students are awarded a nationally recognised City and Guilds Record of Achievements.

RSA Examinations Board

RSA offers a full range of qualifications including National Vocational Qualifications, General National Vocational Qualifications and subject examinations in the following areas:
- Business
- Financial services
- Information technology
- Languages
- Office skills
- Manufacturing
- Retail, wholesale and warehousing

. . . and there are more courses on offer that you might like to consider. Your careers officer will be able to help you find out about them.

BTEC programmes at 16+

Level	BTEC First Qualifications (equivalent to NVQ Level 2)	BTEC National Qualifications (equivalent to NVQ Level 3)
Entry Point	No formal examination passes stipulated by BTEC but some centres ask for GCSEs.	• BTEC First Certificate or Diploma • 4 GCSEs grade C or better • CPVE or Foundation Programme with suitable attainment • other equivalent qualification.
Description	Initial vocational qualifications for those who have chosen the key areas they want to work in. Students develop essential skills which provide a foundation for work or further study.	Nationally recognised qualification for technicians and administrators.
Normal Duration	1 year part-time First Certificate 1 year full-time } First Diploma 2 years part-time }	2 years part-time National Certificate 2 years full-time } National Diploma 3 years part-time }
Equivalent to*	} Several O levels/GCSEs	GCSE A-level (The BTEC National is accepted as a standard route to degree courses subject to obtaining the right grades.)

* Because of the vocational nature of BTEC programmes, it is not always appropriate to compare BTEC qualifications to other purely academic qualifications. However, in this column we list the generally accepted equivalent standards for guidance only.

These qualifications will be phased out as BTEC General National Vocational Qualifications take their place. BTEC GNVQ level 3 is a standard comparable to A-level.

Programmes are available in the following areas:

Built Environment
Computing & Information Systems
Design
Engineering
Land and Countryside
Service and Caring

Business & Finance and
   Public Administration
Distribution, Hotel &
   Catering, Leisure & Tourism
Management Education &
   Training

DIPLOMA *of*
VOCATIONAL
EDUCATION

City and Guilds
of London Institute

Module Summary

LEVEL   Intermediate
NAME   Peter Smith
CENTRE   Hometown High School
MODULE TITLE   Providing Business Services   TYPE   Introductory

Description of work and achievements demonstrated

This module covered a range of business games and simulations and included an introduction to word processing and to the range of employment opportunities available locally in the business and administrative field.

Communication and Social Skills
I interviewed people in two local firms which has helped me to talk to strangers more easily. I also arranged two visits by telephone successfully.

Applied Numeracy
I was told about stocks and shares and did a range of assignments so that I could learn how to use and log petty cash.

Problem-Solving
I did a number of group problem-solving exercises using straws and paper to build a shelter.

Science, Technology and Information Technology
I used Edword and Amstrad Locoscript word processing packages. The firms I visited showed me the range of technology they used.

Social, Industrial and Economic Awareness
I helped with a survey of the local area about opportunities available for a school leaver in Business Administration. I was surprised to discover all the different sorts of jobs that were available.

Vocational Skills Developed
Basic skills in word processing and clerical services, including writing, editing and printing documents and using the telephone.

Signed (Student)   Date
Signed (Tutor)   Date

City and Guilds
of London Institute

This Record of Achievement towards

THE DIPLOMA OF VOCATIONAL EDUCATION

is awarded to MICHAEL OWEN

WHO ATTENDED UPTOWN COLLEGE

AND DEVELOPED SKILLS IN THE FOLLOWING AREAS:

COMMUNICATION AND SOCIAL SKILLS
APPLIED NUMERACY PROBLEM-SOLVING
SCIENCE, TECHNOLOGY AND INFORMATION TECHNOLOGY
SOCIAL, INDUSTRIAL AND ECONOMIC AWARENESS

AND SUCCESSFULLY COMPLETED THE FOLLOWING MODULES:

PROVIDING GOODS AND SERVICES;
   TRANSPORTING – (WORK EXPERIENCE)
PROVIDING GOODS AND SERVICES;
   TRANSPORTING (INTRODUCTORY)
PROVIDING TRAVEL AND TOURISM SERVICES (EXPLORATORY)
CUSTOMER SERVICE (PREPARATORY)
TRAVEL AGENCY SERVICES (PREPARATORY)
GEOGRAPHY OF TOURISM (PREPARATORY)
FRENCH FOR WORK (PREPARATORY)
WORD PROCESSING (PREPARATORY)
DATABASES (PREPARATORY)

Awarded JUNE 1992

Reference No.

John A Barnes

Director-General

A certificate is awarded to candidates who complete the required list of achievements

The City and Guilds of London Institute is incorporated by Royal Charter and was founded in 1878.

RO1

98

A possible way forward to 17+

The precise subjects making up your one-year sixth-form experience can only be decided when:
- your fifth-year results are known
- you have discussed the possibilities with your sixth-year course adviser.

That does not mean to say, however, that you should avoid the issue all through year five. Start looking out for what is on offer and see which parts could be tailor-made for you. The detailed possibilities are endless; the broad way forward will probably look something like this:

English and maths
+
One or two other GCSE subjects
+
Careers counselling
+
Life and vocational skills training
+
Leisure pursuits
+
Work experience
+
Confidence-building activities
+
The CPVE Certificate or similar
=
Better employment chances

So, one year or two, is the sixth form for you?

In every decision we make there are points for and against. Going on to the sixth form is no exception. Look at the pair of scales below. ADVANTAGES are weighed against DISADVANTAGES and they look to be in balance. Their true weight, however, is a very personal business. Consider each item and see which way the scales tip.

1 Continuity of staff you know (if an 11–18 school).	1 Could be thought of as more of the same – time for a complete change.
2 Continuity of subjects and familiarity of teaching methods.	2 Not a good 'buy' if no one is really recommending it.
3 Programme of subjects which fit your previous options.	3 Insufficient financial support when compared with a wage or even a grant.
4 Special courses for particular purposes.	4 Staying on could make you too old for some training opportunities.
5 General studies – a valuable non-exam extra.	5 Other vocational courses, being purpose-built, are more attractive.
6 Small classes with personal attention and counselling from experts on social issues and careers chances.	6 The sixth form (in school) still has a lot of younger people about. You may wish to appear grown-up and be free of them.
7 An active social life with friends on the same course.	
8 Free books and equipment (in school).	

ADVANTAGES   DISADVANTAGES

If the answer were YES, what should I expect?

It is natural at this stage for some to look upon the prospect of further study with a somewhat jaundiced eye. If at this moment you are caught up in the pressures of GCSE examinations, there are some specific points you can look forward to.

Sixth-form characteristics

● The sixth form, whether it is in a school or a college, is not a rest cure, but neither is it a continuation of the sort of pressures which precede a multi-subject examination like GCSE.

● You should have a chance to specialise, ie drop the subjects you find more difficult and concentrate in depth upon those you enjoy.

● Considerable freedom and responsibility will be given to you in the way you work. Your teaching groups are likely to be small and, as such, they are likely to become more like discussion groups between you and the staff.

● There are opportunities for personal development in terms of leadership and responsibility which are not provided for students elsewhere.

Increasing numbers of students staying on for GCE A-level, together with rising standards of entry to higher education and top-level training schemes, give A-level work a prominence and prestige which is not going to diminish. Passes at A-level provide keys which open doors to a very wide range of higher education opportunities – and not only at universities. **Those of you who are advised that you could manage A-level work should not ignore the opportunity.**

For some of you, the appeal of the sixth form will not be in the field of careers at all. You will want to move on to the sixth because you enjoy your work in particular subjects – as simple as that – and have no formulated career plans at all. Most schools would regard this as a very acceptable reason for staying on, but if you are one of these people, make sure your subject choices will leave you as many options as possible after finishing. Study for study's sake is excellent but an ill-considered sixth-form choice could limit career openings later.

If the answer were YES, where would I go?

So far in this book we have been talking about the sixth form, or 16+ as it is beginning more widely to be called, as if opportunities existed only in your own school.

Education opportunities after 16 may vary according to where you live. In some areas you can stay on at school. In others you would move to a sixth-form college. This chapter looks at the opportunities to be found in either. In other parts of the country, all education and training is combined in tertiary colleges or colleges of further education. In these cases, read chapters five and six as one. Note, however, that where you study is less important than the successful outcome of the right course.

The answer

There are so many 'ifs' and 'buts' about the whole business of staying on. The answer must be an individual one and no one can have the responsibility of deciding for you. So, make it personal and get it into focus by giving a straight YES or NO to the questions below.

	Yes	No
Could I study one, two or three subjects to GCE A-level?		
Has my career choice an age of entry at 18+ and 21+?		
Am I interested in higher education – university, polytechnic or college?		
Would I gain socially from the sixth form?		
Are there subjects which I previously dropped and would like to take up again?		
Is there a time gap to fill usefully before going on to the next stage?		
Would a spell in the sixth fill the gap before the right job comes up?		
Could I succeed with more GCSE subjects?		
Are there new subjects which attract me?		
Is there evidence of a preference for 18+entry in the career area of my choice?		

Score three or more YES responses and the sixth form is for you.

Qualifications around the corner

Education never stands still. Because the skills set out on pages 74–5 are regarded as so important, it is possible that reforms in the 16–19 field will mean that the academic/vocational gap as far as qualifications are concerned will be permanently bridged.

If this happens, it is likely to stem from the influence of a body you will hear more about in the future – the NCVQ (**The National Council for Vocational Qualifications**). It is a government body responsible for developing a rational approach to vocational qualifications – bringing the various contributors to the scene into one meaningful whole – level for level. Each NVQ (National Vocational Qualification) thus established will represent a level of competence which is regarded not only as directly useful for employers as a gauge to the level of skill on which they can rely but also, for you, as a basis for going forward to the next level – a system in which you can accumulate your credits.

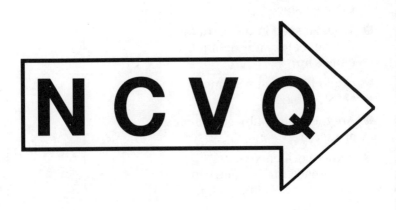

NVQ Level	Broad level of skill	Example of vocational qualification	Example of academic qualification
1	Competence in a range of routine and predictable operations of a practical nature.	Specialist skills certification	A modest range of GCSEs likely to be grades below C
2	Competence in a broader and more demanding range of work activities than level one.	BTEC first certificate and many City & Guilds certificates	Five GCSE grades A to C
3	Competence in skilled areas in a wide range of activities which are both complex and non-routine. May involve supervision of other people.	BTEC National Diploma	Five GCSE grades A to C (or better) and Two GCE A-levels (or more)
4	Competence in complex specialised technical and professional work activities including designing, planning and problem-solving.	BTEC Higher National Diploma	Diploma in Higher Education (DipHE)
5	Competence at the highest levels of technology, professionalism and abstraction. Responsibility for management, supervision and accountability paramount.	Professional institute examinations	University or polytechnic degree

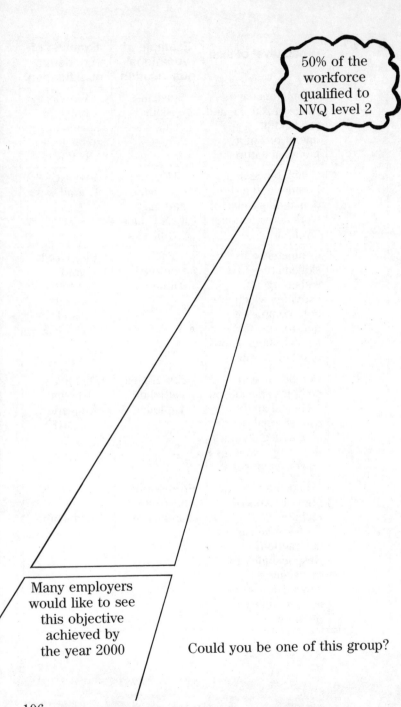

You choose – training now and work later?

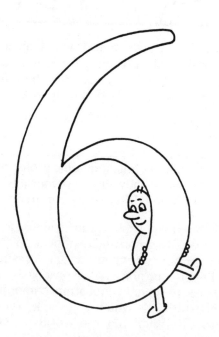

Careerwise, do you know where you are going?

If you know exactly which way you hope to go for your career and wish to start training for it at 16 or 17, then this is the chapter for you. There are ideas here to help you get hold of the Q factor discussed in chapter 2.

Watch out

> While technical qualifications are immensely useful, they are not always transferable between different career areas.

This means that if you wish to start training as a hairdresser, there are courses to go on and qualifications to get. Become trained and you can expect a hairdressing firm to be interested in you, but not a baker or a pastry cook – even if the course has a general education component in it. You may have artistic skills which you think you could transfer from one to the other, but the world of work is not yet flexible enough to see it that way.

This chapter is for the clear-headed, single-minded 16+ students who know where they are going.

Where to go

Most of the careers courses you can consider are based at a college of further education (sometimes called 'the tech'). Such colleges are often very different from school in a number of ways:

● All the students there are 16 or over in age. ● Everyone there is a voluntary member. ● The atmosphere is usually less closely regulated than that of school (eg no uniform). ● The teaching methods are on adult lines. ● Equipment is often more sophisticated than that of school. ● Student activities are sometimes very enterprising. ● Teachers (called lecturers) often have direct experience of industry and commerce.	**COLLEGE ADVANTAGES**

There are possible snags:

● The freer atmosphere means that a lot of self-discipline will be required from you. ● The presence of part-time students can reduce the community spirit. ● Student activities are usually self-started; if there is apathy about, they don't exist. ● You will be expected to learn in an adult way. ● You may have to pay for your courses if you are over 18. ● If you don't work or if you cause undue 'hassle' you could be asked to leave. ● A college is not likely to look after you in so all-embracing a way as a school; help will be around but it will be up to you to ask for it. ● You may have to travel further to college than you did to school.	**COLLEGE DISADVANTAGES**

So weigh it up, and if you think you are interested, read on!

What's in a name?

As of April 1993 these colleges will effectively be limited companies and you may find them called a whole range of different names, operating under the general label of:

Further education

Tertiary college	Technical college	College of art	College of agriculture
An all-in-one college for the whole 16+ student population combining sixth-form courses and further education in one community	A further education college specialising in business studies, science and technology	A further education college specialising in training for a wide range of graphic and design skills	A specialist college for those going to work on the land – farming, horticulture, poultry-keeping and forestry

You can find other examples across the country, especially where a local industry is dominant and has a particular flavour to it, eg seamanship, engineering, textiles. There are about 600 further education colleges, so you will find many varieties.

How are the courses organised?

The arrangements for studying at these colleges are mainly of three kinds.

● **Going all day every day – full-time students**

● **Going for a day or part of a day each week – part-time students**

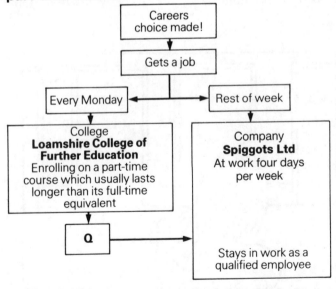

- **Going for solid periods of time sandwiched between periods of full-time work – block-release students**

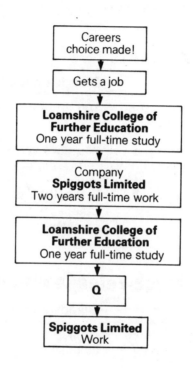

Careers choice made!

↓

Gets a job

↓

Loamshire College of Further Education
One year full-time study

Company Spiggots Limited
Two years full-time work

Loamshire College of Further Education
One year full-time study

↓

Q

↓

Spiggots Limited
Work

COLLEGE   COMPANY

The patterns of courses will vary considerably depending on a number of factors, such as:
- the way that the industry sees the training
- the nature of the skills to be learned
- the capacity of the college to cope.

There are advantages and disadvantages of each method of training.

Full-time students

Advantages	Disadvantages
You can soak yourself in the course more fully.	You are not paid.
The course builds up a community spirit.	You have yet to find a job.
You are not tied to one employer.	You will have wasted a lot of time if your career choice changes.

Part-time/block-release students

Advantages	Disadvantages
You are paid throughout your work and training.	It takes longer to get the qualifications.
You can connect theory with practice.	You may feel that the theory gets in the way of the practice.
Your studies are not too intensively arranged.	You may feel less committed to the college.

What is on offer?

The exact nature of the courses offered will depend on a number of local factors, but following is a small representative selection of courses found across the country.

It must be appreciated, however, that this list is only a tiny fraction of what is on offer, and is shown here to give examples of what may be found. Only approximate entry requirements are shown since they may be subject to local variations.

Courses for school-leavers who are good with their hands

Course	Length	Approximate entry requirements	Award
General engineering	1 or 2 years	3/4 GCSE grades A to C	BTEC National Certificate
Agriculture	1 year	No formal qualifications but GCSE grades A to C in English, maths or science preferred, plus practical experience	College Award
Building studies	2 or 3 years	4 GCSE grades A to C	BTEC National Diploma
Radio, TV and electronic engineering	1 year	A good general education	College Award

Courses for school-leavers who are artistic

Course	Length	Approximate entry requirements	Award
Graphics and visual communications	2 years	4 GCSE grades A to C. Evidence of talent	BTEC National Diploma
Drama	2 years	3/4 GCSE grades A to C. Evidence of talent	GCE A-levels and College Diploma
Designer for printing	3 years	GCSE grades A to C in art and English	CGLI Certificate
Photography	1 year	5 GCSE grades A to C	College Award

Courses for school-leavers who are interested in social care

Course	Length	Approximate entry requirements	Award
Pre-nursing	1 year	As locally required	GCSEs
Nursery nursing	2 years	GCSE grades A to C in English and 3 or 4 supporting subjects desirable	Certificate of the Nursery Nurses Examinations Board
Home management and family care	2 years	4 GCSE grades A to C	Certificate of the National Council for Home Economics Education
Dental surgery assistance	1 year plus, p/t	2 GCSE grades A to C	Dental Surgery Assistant Certificate

Courses for school-leavers who are interested in business organisation and management

Course	Length	Approximate entry requirements	Award
Business studies with special option, eg languages, secretarial	2 years	4 GCSE grades A to C	BTEC National Diploma
Hotel reception	1 year	2 GCSE grades A to C	CGLI Certificate
Hotel catering and institutional management	1 year	3/4 GCSE grades A to C	BTEC National Diploma
Clerk/typist	1 year	a good general education	RSA typing

Now check with your local college of further education to see what is available to you.

What do you get at the end?

The final column of the charts sets out the qualifications which are obtainable at the end of the course. They vary considerably. The principal ones are:

General Certificate of Secondary Education GCE A-level	The same qualifications as you have and can obtain at school. They are achieved through studies which are not especially careers-slanted, ie you can use them for any career.

CGLI	The City and Guilds of London Institute, which awards certificates in its own right, usually for craft or operative courses. Each course has an identifying number after it for easy recognition, eg CG 156.

BTEC	BTEC is the Business and Technology Education Council, offering nationally recognised qualifications in a wide range of subjects – agriculture and related subjects, business and finance, computing and information systems, construction, design and art, engineering, public administration and distribution.
	Courses can be studied by a number of different methods and there are four main categories of certificate and diploma award – general, national, higher national certificate (part-time) or diploma (full-time) and post experience. The first two are for 16+ students, the others 18+.

RSA	The Royal Society of Arts is both a qualification awarding body in a wide range of vocational skills and a research institution enquiring into future employment trends.

Too high-powered?

Maybe all the suggestions listed above are too high-powered for you. Perhaps you have not yet decided exactly what you want to do. It could be that you would like to do some sampling of the world of work before making up your mind. You may not yet be convinced that you could measure up to two more years of extra study.

Bridging courses

The main features of these courses are:
- they give you work experience
- they can provide special skills training
- they improve your confidence to cope
- they give you a useful breathing space after school to prepare for employment
- they provide you with cash allowances during training
- they can last for two years
- they can give you a vocational qualification

– in short

Youth Training

Technical training for the 1990s

YTS performed a useful service, offering skill training at a time of much unemployment. It helped considerably the chances of finding work in the 1980s – over 70% success rates in securing permanent work in some areas were reported.

The 1990s have already offered new challenges. The recession has meant school-leavers have again found it difficult to find employment. Training has never before been so important.

The opportunity has been taken to involve industry and education in a new partnership.

TRAINING AND ENTERPRISE COUNCILS

Tecs for short.

While this is not a happy abbreviation, because of the possible confusion which may arise with techs (local technical colleges), it is important to understand their place in your future.

Who is behind the Tecs?

● Tecs were set up by the Government. They were first announced in a government White Paper called *Employment for the 1990s*.

● Your local Tec is made up of leading industrialists in the area (who will know what training needs exist) and local educationalists (who will have ideas about how these needs can be met).

● Other groups in the community also form part of a Tec, so that everyone concerned about the availability and quality of training in a given locality has an opportunity of contributing to its policy and programme of activities.

What are Tecs for?

● Their principal job is to make sure that the local labour force has the right skills and attitudes to make industry in the area efficient and competitive for the expanding markets of Europe, and for anticipated changes which will come from more flexible manufacturing processes.

● It will agree on providing training to improve the education and training of its workforce for its own benefit.

● The business partnership which it represents should make for the best possible opportunities for all concerned – raising the UK from its present position as one of the lowest participators in higher education in the Western world.

What kind of training will these Tecs offer?

YT is the programme of training. It offers a broad training, with particular emphasis being placed on vocational qualifications.

What is it for?

Anyone is eligible and you can start at any age. The only exceptions are likely to be higher education students, students still at school and foreign nationals requiring work permits. Under-18s can enter the scheme as many times as they like. Over-18s, however, have one opportunity.

How long does it last?

It will be more a question of how long will it take before you get yourself qualified.

Everyone starting will have a personal plan which will be aimed at achieving NVQ level 2 (see p124).

What support do I get?

Everyone undergoing training will receive an allowance which is likely to be £29.50 per week for those in year one, rising to £35.00 in the second year.

There is also special support (not of a financial kind) for those who find learning particularly difficult. Ask your careers officer if you think this may affect you.

What will training offer me?

YT schemes may differ both across the country and according to the occupations they serve and reflect. There are, however, some common factors built in to all courses and you should be aware of these before you decide whether a YT course is for you. Some of the important common elements are:

Planned programme

Each scheme will start with a planned programme to help you to assess your own needs. Knowing where you are going is half-way to getting there.

Off-the-job training

Some skills are best learnt away from the place of work. The theory, the ideas, the discussion and reading will be provided in a separate establishment, but will be related to your practical experience.

Planned work experience

This is learning by doing – trying your hand at a real job for a set period in a real work environment. This can be at one place of work or with a number of companies.

Guidance and support

You are not left to get by on your own. A particular member of the training staff will be reviewing your progress on a regular basis, so there is no doubt as to how you are getting on.

Basic skills

Whichever occupation your scheme reflects, opportunities will be given to you to make progress in five basic areas:

- numbers and their application
- communication
- problem-solving and planning
- manual dexterity
- computer literacy and information technology

ALL TRAINING LEADING YOU TO A VOCATIONAL QUALIFICATION

Equivalent to NVQ level 2 or 3

Whatever sorts of schemes are available to you, all programmes are likely to include:

● a personal training plan

● written details of what the scheme involves

● direct practical experience

● training in a group of skills related to an area of work

● some useful lifeskills

● help and advice about how to make the best use of the scheme in the future

● a certificate of achievement at the end

● an opportunity to work for a vocational qualification.

What's all this about Training Credits?

By 1996 Training Credits will be one of the main ways TECs fund training for young people entering the workforce. There are already a number of training credit pilots. It may be that you are in an area where a pilot scheme has been set up. Your local careers office will know about this.

What is a Training Credit?

It is a sum of money allocated to you in the workplace. Training must lead to a nationally recognised qualification. At the moment all training credit pilots are different because they are geared to the needs of local labour market – which means there should be a job for you at the end of your training.

What will I earn?

If you are an employee of the organisation you are working in, you will get the rate for the job. You may need to pay tax and national insurance. If you are in a training placement you will receive the training allowance already mentioned. However, many employers pay more than this.

How does it work?

The general idea is that you and your employer 'own' your training. The type of qualification, method, pace and place of your training will reflect your needs and your employer's requirements.

You will be able to find help with other training needs such as reading, writing and maths, if you think this will help you gain your qualifications, and perform in a specific job.

If you have a disability, you should be able to find help with the adaption of your workplace premises.

Local TEC delivery of Training Credits

The following are likely to be offered whichever pilot scheme you join:

- Help with finding a training placement or job
- Careers guidance
- A training plan based on your needs and those of your employer
- Planned training leading to a nationally recognised qualification

The current eleven training credit pilots are run by:

Bradford and District TEC

Birmingham TEC

Devon and Cornwall TEC

Grampian Enterprise Limited

Hertfordshire TEC

Kent TEC

North East Wales TEC

Northumberland TEC

South East Cheshire TEC

South London TEC (SOLO TEC)

Suffolk TEC

Occupationally based training

Whichever scheme you look at, you will find reference made to broadly based occupational training. This is important because it is intended to equip you for a variety of jobs in as wide a field as possible.

Jobs have been grouped, not according to their usual labels like engineering, surveying, hairdressing, etc, but into families according to the kind of *activity* at work. The exact routine of that activity will affect the sort of training you get. For example:

Activity
Making small objects by using hand or power tools

Training in
Hand skills
Power tool operation
Safety at work
Advertising
Accountancy
etc

Job examples
Potter
Bookbinder
Woodcarver
Jewellery-maker
etc

This approach is known as learning in **Occupational Training Families** or OTF for short.

Occupationally based training

OTF no	Occupations	Key purpose
1	Administrative, clerical and office services	Information processing
2	Agriculture, horticulture, forestry and fisheries	Nurturing and gathering living resources
3	Craft and design	Creating single or small numbers of objects using hand or power tools
4	Installation, maintenance and repair	Applying known procedures for making equipment work
5	Technical and scientific	Applying known principles to make things work or usable
6	Manufacturing and assembly	Transforming metallic and non-metallic materials through shaping, constructing and assembling into products
7	Processing	Intervening into the working of machines when necessary
8	Food preparation and service	Transforming and handling edible matter
9	Personal service and sales	Satisfying the needs of individual customers
10	Community and health services	Meeting the socially defined needs of the community
11	Transport services	Moving goods and people

Words of warning . . .

It must be pointed out, however, that YT is not the answer to everyone's needs. There are aspects of it which should be carefully considered, as with all post-16 routes. The following points are offered, not as a condemnation of the scheme, but as issues for reflection before taking the plunge.

. . . About the courses

In no way can YT be seen as a continuing, broadly based general education. At school, students have social education lessons, which give the opportunity of discussing views on political issues, moral problems and controversial current affairs.

Don't ignore the other tried and tested avenues which stretch out from 16+. Some places run their own vocational courses in the sixth form which combine the best features of YT with a good broad sixth-form education and enjoy a high permanent job record. This could be a better proposition. Above all, if you are recommended to stay on for A-levels because your teachers believe you can succeed, don't go for a YT scheme at any price (even if you would like the £29.50 a week).

YT could eventually take you into higher education but it could be a more difficult route than A-level.

The moral of all this is that no two people are alike. Don't jump on to any bandwagon because you see other people doing it. Consider all the issues; weigh them up with your parents and advisers – then decide.

What do the customers say? Here are a few comments made by first-generation YT students:

I was not keen on the YT compulsory off-the-job courses

I am doing well and learning fast. I enjoyed woodwork at school but had not enough time to do it well

It's great

You learn a lot more to do with the world by actually working

At school you get qualifications, on YT you got experience

Could do with better pay

If you aren't careful, you can be taken advantage of

I would recommend it for everyone who has not put in for the sixth

When you are at work you become more independent

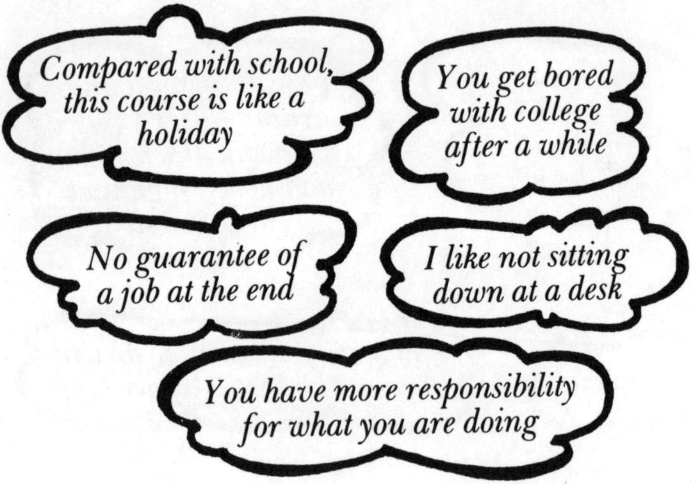
Compared with school, this course is like a holiday
You get bored with college after a while
No guarantee of a job at the end
I like not sitting down at a desk
You have more responsibility for what you are doing

Getting that job

Get yourself started

Finding a job is a demanding process and you can get yourself into a mess unless you are thoroughly organised. With regard to vacancies, you will no doubt be chasing several at once and you will need the skill of a competent juggler. You may have read of one or two in the press; some will be suggested by the careers service; one or two may come from school; the Yellow Pages may give you some more lines of enquiry. It would be easy to get into a mess. Put some method into it and draw up a chart of how your applications progress.

Job	Source	Date of appli-cation	Date of reply	Date of interview	Notes
1					
2					
3					
4					

Chart the progress of each one, so that you avoid a muddle.

With regard to yourself, draw up a full picture of yourself and your life so far.

- Get the dates right.
- Set out your qualifications in full.
- List your spare-time activities, eg swimming, first-aid, music qualifications.

All this information is called a curriculum vitae (Latin for how your life has run) – sometimes abbreviated to cv. Then get your references arranged by asking at least two people to be prepared to answer questions about you from interested employers.

Your record of achievement

During your life so far, you will probably have accumulated a number of documents about yourself and your achievements. They could include:
- Red Cross certificates
- music awards
- examination certificates
- sporting awards
- letters of praise or congratulation
- school awards.

Buy a self-mounting photograph album and arrange the information in a logical order ready to take to interview. If you go around with this and had it to your interviewer, you will be spared the embarrassment of talking about yourself and he or she will have something to talk about. You will have been building up an official school record of achievement. This will now become really important.

Communicating

There is a vacancy in town. You want to be considered for it. This is the art of getting noticed. Many people will be ignored because they messed up their letter of application. Don't let this happen to you. Here are a few tips:

- Choose your notepaper carefully (avoid strong colours, lines, scent and odd shapes).
- Be careful with your layout.
- Use your best handwriting.
- Don't go on and on – they won't read it.
- Use a dictionary if your spelling is risky.

  This is the pattern it could take:

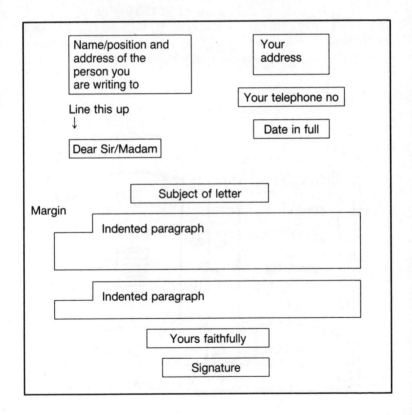

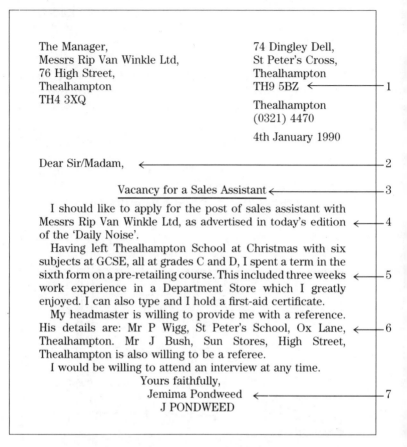

The Manager,
Messrs Rip Van Winkle Ltd,
76 High Street,
Thealhampton
TH4 3XQ

74 Dingley Dell,
St Peter's Cross,
Thealhampton
TH9 5BZ ← 1

Thealhampton
(0321) 4470

4th January 1990

Dear Sir/Madam, ← 2

<u>Vacancy for a Sales Assistant</u> ← 3

I should like to apply for the post of sales assistant with Messrs Rip Van Winkle Ltd, as advertised in today's edition ← 4 of the 'Daily Noise'.

Having left Thealhampton School at Christmas with six subjects at GCSE, all at grades C and D, I spent a term in the sixth form on a pre-retailing course. This included three weeks ← 5 work experience in a Department Store which I greatly enjoyed. I can also type and I hold a first-aid certificate.

My headmaster is willing to provide me with a reference. His details are: Mr P Wigg, St Peter's School, Ox Lane, ← 6 Thealhampton. Mr J Bush, Sun Stores, High Street, Thealhampton is also willing to be a referee.

I would be willing to attend an interview at any time.

Yours faithfully,
Jemima Pondweed ← 7
J PONDWEED

There are several points to stress here:

1 Make sure your address is written in full and that it includes the correct postcode. Guessing it won't do. An inaccurate one could cause a missort at the post office and you might receive a request to attend an interview too late. It has happened!

2 Dear Sir or Madam? It is not a bad idea to find out who you are writing to. A careful telephone call to the company without bothering the manager could sort that out for you.

3 The title or subject of the letter may be obvious to you but, remember, 60 letters or more may arrive with yours. You don't want yours misfiled. So, be clear.

4 Be clear and positive.

5 If you can say something new, it is worth it. You want your letter to stand out in comparison with others, so look at what you are offering to see if there is something distinctive.

6 Always ask your referees' permission before quoting them.

7 Sign your name clearly. Don't use a 'flashy' signature. Print your name beneath only if necessary.

It is worth making several attempts to get it right, or else . . .

The interview

If you get an interview, you are well on the way. The task now is to persuade the interviewer that you are just the right person the firm is looking for. Once again, this is a strategy worth taking time and trouble over.

Feeling threatened?
Be convinced that no interviewer wants to scare you.

It is not in their interests to do so. He or she will be looking for the best person to fit the company's needs, and you will be considering if the firm is the best place for you. The successful interview is one where there is a good fit on both sides.

Nervous?
It is perfectly natural to go off quaking in your shoes.

You need to get on top of it, however, when the interview starts. Be direct, straightforward and, above all, honest. Don't pretend to have experience you have not got.

Be prepared

Find out about the company before you go. Travel to the place of interview the day before, to get the timing right. Don't be late or you will get flustered. Remember the Chinese proverb: 'He who starts late, trots all day.'

Take your book of achievements with you.

Dress appropriately

No one will expect you to look like a dog's dinner.

They will expect you to look clean and tidy, wearing clothes which are appropriate for the interview or for the work you may be doing. Remember, you may be interviewed by someone a quarter of a century older than you. Their idea of good gear may be different from yours – try to bridge the generation gap sensibly.

Listen well

Make sure you understand what is being asked. Always answer the questions clearly and directly. Don't be evasive. Answer in such a way that the interviewer can pick up a point and reply – like playing tennis.

Start and finish well

Make a good entrance. Don't creep in under the door. Be polite and show confidence. Don't shake hands like a dead fish. Thank the interviewer at the end, however well or badly you think it has gone.

How to improve your interview technique

Questions	Possible answer. True but deadly dull	Possible answer. Better because it gives the interviewer something to go on
Which school did you attend?	Thealhampton	St Peter's, Thealhampton until part-way through the sixth form
When did you leave?	Christmas	Christmas, after taking two GCSEs in November
What exams have you passed?	GCSEs	English D, maths C, biology E, geography E, art B, home ec B
What are your interests?	Pigeons	Pigeon-keeping – at least it was until the cat got into the pigeon-house
How did your work experience go?	All right	All right, though I found some of the customers awkward
Why do you want this job?	I'm short of cash	I enjoyed my work experience in spite of the problems. I want to do retailing properly and be paid for it!

Next Monday . . .

Rip Van Winkle Ltd

High Street, Thealhampton TH4 3XQ

18th January 1990

Miss J Pondweed
74 Dingley Dell
St Peter's Cross
Thealhampton TH9 5BZ

Dear Miss Pondweed,
    Thank you for attending our interview last Thursday. I am
sorry to have to tell you that we are unable to offer you a
post in the company.

Yours sincerely,
T. Bunkum
Manager

So it did not come off – this time. What next?

A few ideas

Get the disappointment into *perspective*.
The response that you get is not necessarily
a reflection on you as a person. You must
not feel diminished by it. The fact of the
matter is that Mr Bunkum probably
received applications from 50 individuals,
23 of whom would have been acceptable
for the job. And that includes you. So cheer
up – it's not you that's wrong, it's only that
the competition is too fierce.

Don't give up after one or even many refusals. *Try, try and try again.* The whole business of seeking jobs and landing one is not subject to any rules. What makes for rejection in one place and an acceptance in another is a curious, unpredictable chemistry of people and places. Above all, don't try to draw any logical conclusions, like, 'If they won't have me at A, there's no chance for B'. There is *no* logic about it. Each application is a one-off attempt.

If you are getting depressed about the job scene, join a *support group.* In many places, especially in the cities, there are centres for the unemployed, often based in youth clubs. Being with others in the same boat could lighten the burden. Support groups can be valuable morale boosters.

Get the most out of your *careers service.* Keep closely in touch with your careers officer so that you are in contact when the odd vacancy does come in. Tell them in the careers office about your movements (like holidays). You and your careers officer can work like partners on the problem, but a great deal must be up to you. He or she cannot be a wet-nurse, neither can they magic up vacancies.

If you are reading this before leaving school, make sure your *school record*, which will be reflected in your references, is as good as it possibly can be. Employers take notice of it and a good one can work miracles. It may mean putting more beef into your work and pulling your weight in out-of-school activities. Don't be put off by rumours that, because jobs are hard to get, school success is unimportant. That is misleading nonsense.

Try *advertising* your skills. You have a clear idea of what you can offer. Set out what you want on an attractive card and advertise your wares in a local shop's information box. You may be surprised at what turns up.

Take advantage of as much *leisure activity* as you can. Whatever your interests are, practise them positively during the waiting period. This will be far better than moping about at home or staying in bed. It beats the boredom of unemployment to be active.

Take the opportunity to have a *rethink*. Are you aiming too high? Are there areas (careers or geographical) where more jobs are available? Are your applications watertight? Get a friend to check them out.

Be prepared to *travel* further from home. The job you want may be available if you are prepared to do this. Too many 16 year-olds want work close to where they live. You may have to look further afield and be more adventurous.

You could even consider setting up your *own company*. Admittedly, capital is hard to come by when you are starting up, but help is sometimes around. The sort of activities worth considering are:
baby-sitting service (with registration)
catering
toy making
window cleaning
gardening
delivery
typing services.
Take advice and think about it.

What can you do with your qualifications?

What can I do with my qualifications?

The table on page 150 has been compiled to give you some idea of the very wide range of careers open to you. Choose the column nearest to the qualifications you hope to gain and then compare the careers open after GCSEs with those open after A-levels. How different are they? Naturally, the table oversimplifies the position: in some areas firms can demand more than the minimum qualifications. Also, there may be special courses at colleges of further education for entrants to local industries.

Before you start using the table, an important word of warning: do not use it for working out precise entrance requirements for careers. Entrance requirements are far too complicated to be tabulated like this; only a rough idea can be gained from the table. If you want to know the entrance requirements, look them up in some up-to-date careers literature. The letters in the first column refer to the Careers Library Classification Index (CLCI) – the method of classifying careers literature used in most schools.

Some GCSEs grades D–G

This is the section where most local variations are likely to appear. Some employers require GCSEs for training schemes or clerical work, whereas in other areas of the country this may be rare. Some careers that are in the table, such as air cabin crew and fashion modelling, have many entrants with GCSEs and A-levels, but these qualifications are not compulsory. Some careers, eg building management, organisation and methods, are commonly entered after a period in some other career for which there are no formal qualifications.

1–3 GCSEs grades A–C and GCSEs grades D–F

Most of the careers in this section require some part-time study, but this is generally for a fairly short time.

4–5 GCSEs grades A–C and further training

Trainees for careers with these qualifications often take a BTEC (Business and Technology Education Council) national qualification. You may have to study part-time at a college of further education for some years. This is also the part-time study route to professional qualifications in engineering, business and science. It is possible to finish with qualifications of the same level as a degree holder, but if you are aiming for degree level from the outset it is better to choose full-time education, as part-time study over a long period is very hard work.

Full-time courses at colleges of further education for BTEC and other qualifications entered at this level generally last for two years. Applicants for courses in farming, horticulture and forestry must have gained some experience before starting their courses. There are BTEC courses in business and finance, construction, hotel and catering, leisure, engineering, distribution, caring, design, science, agriculture, computing and information technology, public administration, travel and tourism and performing arts. A BTEC national certificate or diploma can be followed by further study for a BTEC higher national certificate or diploma. A BTEC with good grades can also be used as an entry qualification to a degree course at a university or polytechnic. Colleges regard it as equivalent to A-levels.

Foundation courses in art and design last for one year and are followed by a three-year CNAA BA degree in art and design. There are also shorter, more vocationally orientated design courses.

GCE A-level qualifications

Choose the column that most nearly approximates to the A-levels you are taking. If they are all arts A-levels, look down the academic A-levels column.

Careers in business, engineering and science often involve taking a BTEC higher national certificate at a local college by part-time study. Some professional careers, eg accountancy, surveying, actuarial work, landscape architecture and patents, are open to A-level leavers who must study part-time whilst employed in a suitable firm. This route to a professional career is taken by very few young people nowadays and the vast majority of entrants are university and polytechnic graduates. The Civil Service, the Post Office, the Armed Services and many industrial companies have special entry schemes for A-level leavers.

If you are planning to take a BTEC higher national diploma course you must have passed one A-level and studied another subject to A-level standard. In the table, careers that have a BTEC HND entry route are listed as requiring only one A-level. Many careers, chartered engineer, for example, have two possible entry routes for the A-level leaver. You can either take a degree, which will require at least two A-levels, or a BTEC HND followed by courses leading to the examinations of the Engineering Council. The second route will require one A-level and another subject studied to that level. Nowadays most entrants follow the degree route.

Full-time post – A-level higher education

For some careers a degree course is essential, eg architecture, dentistry, medicine, pharmacy, teaching, veterinary work and ophthalmic optics. For other careers you must have taken a full-time course after sixth-form study: examples of such careers include physiotherapy, radiography and occupational therapy.

Expanding your career possibilities

Either:
Start with your qualifications (real or possible), and run down the chart to see what suggestions are made.

Or:
Begin with career areas which interest you, and read along to the left to check what they require in terms of qualifications.

Either way, time spent now on this chart, could focus your career planning in a very positive way.

Knowing where you are going is the first step to getting there.

To sum it all up

Which way for you?

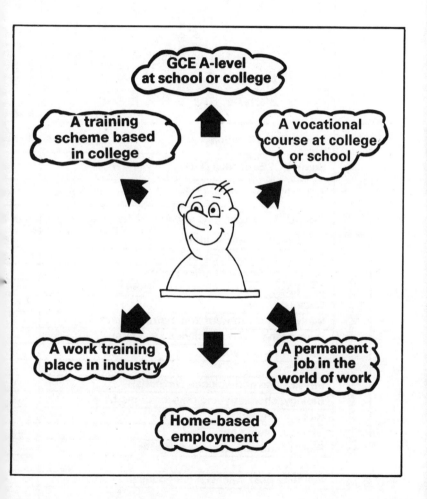

		Accountant	Accountancy technician	Actor
	Note: A = available for this career E = essential for this career G = there is a graduate entry to this career although there are no directly relevant post-A-level courses			
	Library Classification	Nab	Nab	Gab
GCSE qualifications	Some GCSEs grades D–G			●
	1–3 GCSEs grades A–C and GCSEs grades D–F			
	4–5 GCSEs grades A–C and further training	●	●	●
GCE Advanced-level qualifications	Any one academic A-level			●
	Two or more academic A-levels	●	●	
	Chemistry, physics and/or maths			
	Chemistry and non-science subjects			
	Chemistry			
	Maths, physics and/or 2nd maths subject			
	Pure maths and non-science subject(s)			
	One maths subject			
	Physics			
	Physics and non-science subject(s)			
	Biology, chemistry and physics or maths			
	Biology, physics			
	Biology, chemistry			
	Biology and non-science subject(s)			
	Biology			
	Full-time post-A-level higher education course	A		
	Additional notes			

Career	Code	Level
Aero-engine fitter	Rab	(see Engineering)
Aeronautical engineer	Rab	(see Engineering)
Agricultural engineer	Rad	(see Engineering)
Agricultural mechanic	Rad	A
Agriculture	Wab	
Airbroker	Yas	
Air cabin crew	Yab	
Air Force: commissioned	Bal	
Air Force: non-commissioned	Bam	
Aircraft maintenance	Bab	G
Air traffic control: officer	Yab	E †
Air traffic control: assistant	Yab	
Ambulance work	Joc	
Animal technician	Wal	
Antique dealer	Ofm	
Archaeologist	Fag	E
Architectural technician	Ub	
Architect	Ub	E
Archivist	Fag	E
Army: commissioned	Baf	G
Army: non-commissioned	Bag	A
Artist	E	E
Assembly work	S	
Astronomer	Qof	E
Auctioneer	Um	A

essential

† one A-level must be maths, geography or a science subject

		Note: A = available for this career E = essential for this career G = there is a graduate entry to this career although there are no directly relevant post-A-level courses	Audiology technician	Audiotypist	Baking process work	Baking technologist	Ballet
		Library Classification	Job	Cav	Sab	Sab	Gaf
GCSE qualifications		Some GCSEs grades D–G			●		●
		1–3 GCSEs grades A–C and GCSEs grades D–F			●		●
		4–5 GCSEs grades A–C and further training	●	●	●	●	
GCE Advanced-level qualifications		Any one academic A-level					●
		Two or more academic A-levels					●
		Chemistry, physics and/or maths				●	
		Chemistry and non-science subjects				●	
		Chemistry				●	
		Maths, physics and/or 2nd maths subject					
		Pure maths and non-science subject(s)					
		One maths subject					
		Physics					
		Physics and non-science subject(s)					
		Biology, chemistry and physics or maths					
		Biology, physics					
		Biology, chemistry					
		Biology and non-science subject(s)					
		Biology					
		Full-time post-A-level higher education course	A				
		Additional notes					

Job	Code
Bar staff	Ic
Beauty therapy	Ik
Biochemist	Qom
Biologist	Qod
Blacksmith	Saw
Bookbinder	Sar
Bookseller	Ofm
Botanist	Qod
Brewing process work	Sab
Brewing technologist	Sab
Bricklayer	Uf
Broadcasting	Gal
Builders' labourer	Uf
Building management	Ud
Building Society work	Naf
Building surveyor	Um
Bus driver or conductor	Yad
Butcher	Ofm
Buyer	Op
Cabinet-maker	Saj
Camera work (film+TV)	Gal
Cardiological technician	Job
Careers officer	Ked
Carpenter	Uf
Carpet fitter	Ofz
Cartographer	Ut
Cashier	Cax
Catering manager	Ib
Catering assistant	Ic
Ceramics craft	Sad

E A E A

G A A A

A E A A

†geography needed for
some courses

153

		Note: A = available for this career; E = essential for this career; G = there is a graduate entry to this career although there are no directly relevant post-A-level courses	Ceramics design	Ceramics technologist	Chef	Chemical engineering: technologist
		Library Classification	Eg	Sad	Ic	Rag
GCSE qualifications		Some GCSEs grades D–G			●	
		1–3 GCSEs grades A–C and GCSEs grades D–F	●		●	
		4–5 GCSEs grades A–C and further training	●	●	●	
GCE Advanced-level qualifications		Any one academic A-level		●		
		Two or more academic A-levels		●		
		Chemistry, physics and/or maths		●		●
		Chemistry and non-science subjects		●		
		Chemistry		●		
		Maths, physics and/or 2nd maths subject		●		
		Pure maths and non-science subject(s)		●		
		One maths subject		●		
		Physics		●		
		Physics and non-science subject(s)		●		
		Biology, chemistry and physics or maths		●		
		Biology, physics		●		
		Biology, chemistry		●		
		Biology and non-science subject(s)		●		
		Biology		●		
		Full-time post-A-level higher education course	A	A		E
		Additional notes				

Qob	Chemistry
Jat	Chiropodist
Gaf	Choreographer
Gan	Cinema attendant
Un	Civil engineer
	Civil Service:
Cab	administrative
Cab	executive
Cav	clerical officer
Cav	clerical assistant
Ic	Cleaner
Cav	Clerical work
Sah	Clothing production
Rob	Coal miner
Maz	Coastguard
Cap	Company secretary
Sar	Compositor
Pad	Computer operator
Pad	Computer programmer
Pad	Computer systems analyst
Ral	Computer engineer
Sab	Confectioner
Cop	Consumer protection
Ic	Cook
Od	Copywriter
Nab	Cost accountant
Yap	Courier
Uv	Crane driver

(see Engineering)
(see Mining)
(see Advertising)
(see Accountant)

†honours degree required

	Note: A = available for this career E = essential for this career G = there is a graduate entry to this career although there are no directly relevant post-A-level courses	Customs and Excise: executive officer	clerical officer	clerical assistant
Library Classification		Cab	Cab	Cab
GCSE qualifications	Some GCSEs grades D–G			
	1–3 GCSEs grades A–C and GCSEs grades D–F			●
	4–5 GCSEs grades A–C and further training			●
GCE Advanced-level qualifications	Any one academic A-level			
	Two or more academic A-levels			●
	Chemistry, physics and/or maths			
	Chemistry and non-science subjects			
	Chemistry			
	Maths, physics and/or 2nd maths subject			
	Pure maths and non-science subject(s)			
	One maths subject			
	Physics			
	Physics and non-science subject(s)			
	Biology, chemistry and physics or maths			
	Biology, physics			
	Biology, chemistry			
	Biology and non-science subject(s)			
	Biology			
	Full-time post-A-level higher education course	G		
	Additional notes			

Job	Code		Level
Darkroom technician	Soz		A
Data processing	Pad		
Dental hygienist	Jaf		E
Dental surgery assistant	Jaf		A
Dental technician	Jaf		
Dentist	Jaf		
Dietician	Jav		
Dispenser (optics)	Jal		
Dispenser (pharmacy)	Jag		
Display work	Et		
Diver	Yaz		A
Domestic worker	Ic		
Dressmaker	Sah		
Driver	Yad		
Economist	Paf		
Electrical engineer	Rak	(see Engineering)	
Electrician	Rak		
Electronic engineer	Ral	(see Engineering)	
Embroiderer	Sah		
Engineer: technologist	R		E
technician	R		
craft	R		
operative	R		
Environmental health	Cop		A
Estate agent	Um		A
Exhibition designer	Et		A
Exporter	Os		A

†most courses require 3 A-levels

157

		Factory inspector	Farm secretary	Farmer	Farrier
	Note: A = available for this career E = essential for this career G = there is a graduate entry to this career although there are no directly relevant post-A-level courses				
	Library Classification	Cot	Cat	Wab	Saw
GCSE qualifications	Some GCSEs grades D–G			●	●
	1–3 GCSEs grades A–C and GCSEs grades D–F		●	●	●
	4–5 GCSEs grades A–C and further training		●	●	
GCE Advanced-level qualifications	Any one academic A-level				
	Two or more academic A-levels				
	Chemistry, physics and/or maths	●		●	
	Chemistry and non-science subjects	●		●	
	Chemistry	●		●	
	Maths, physics and/or 2nd maths subject	●		●	
	Pure maths and non-science subject(s)	●		●	
	One maths subject	●		●	
	Physics	●		●	
	Physics and non-science subject(s)	●		●	
	Biology, chemistry and physics or maths	●		●	
	Biology, physics	●		●	
	Biology, chemistry	●		●	
	Biology and non-science subject(s)	●		●	
	Biology	●		●	
	Full-time post-A-level higher education course	E		A	
	Additional notes				

158

Occupation	Code
Fashion designer	Ej
Fashion model	Ot
Film producer	Gal
Film projectionist	Gan
Fire service	Maf
Fishing	Wag
Florist	Ofm
Forestry:	
forest officer	Waf
forester	Waf
forest worker	Waf
Foundry technology	Sam
Fuel science	Ran
Funeral director	Ip
Furniture design	Eg
Furniture manufacture	Saj
Furniture sales	Ofm
Gamekeeper	War
Game warden	War
Garage mechanic	Rae
Gardener	Wad
Gas engineer	Ran
Gas fitter	Ran
Geologist	Qol
Glazier	Uf
Goldsmith	Eg
Graphic designer	Ed
Greengrocer	Ofm
Grocer	Ofm

(see Engineering)

Interest group markers: A, E, A A, A, E, A

159

		Groundsman	Hairdresser	Health services management	Health visitor	Heating engineer	Helicopter pilot
	Library Classification	Wad	II = Cal	Jad	Uj	Yah	
GCSE qualifications	Some GCSEs grades D–G	●	●				
	1–3 GCSEs grades A–C and GCSEs grades D–F	●	●	●		(see Engineering)	
	4–5 GCSEs grades A–C and further training			●	●		●
GCE Advanced-level qualifications	Any one academic A-level			●	●		
	Two or more academic A-levels				●		
	Chemistry, physics and/or maths						
	Chemistry and non-science subjects						
	Chemistry						
	Maths, physics and/or 2nd maths subject						
	Pure maths and non-science subject(s)						
	One maths subject						
	Physics						
	Physics and non-science subject(s)						
	Biology, chemistry and physics or maths						
	Biology, physics						
	Biology, chemistry						
	Biology and non-science subject(s)						
	Biology						
	Full-time post-A-level higher education course				G	A	
Additional notes							

Note:
A = available for this career
E = essential for this career
G = there is a graduate entry to this career although there are no directly relevant post-A-level courses

Id	Occupation
	Home economist
Wam	Horses, work with
Wad	Horticulture
Sah	Hosiery manufacture
Ib	Hotel management
Cav	Hotel reception
Ic	Hotel work
Um	Housing management
Cab	Immigration officer
Faf	Information science
Ib	Institutional management
Nag	Insurance
Et	Interior designer
Fal	Interpreter
Ofm	Ironmonger
	Jewellery:
Eg	craft
Ofm	retail
Eg	design
Gag	Jockey
Uf	Joiner
Fac	Journalist
Lag	Justice's clerk
Wam	Kennel work
Q	Laboratory technician
Um	Land management
Ul	Landscape architecture
Fal	Languages, work with
Ig	Laundry work
Ed	Layout artist

†must include a language

†must be qualified barrister or solicitor

†must include a language

161

		Note: A = available for this career E = essential for this career G = there is a graduate entry to this career although there are no directly relevant post-A-level courses	Leather technology	Legal work: barrister	legal executive	solicitor	Librarian	Lorry driver	Machinist: engineering	sewing/knitting
	Library Classification		Saf	Lab	Lad	Lac	Faf	Yad	R	Sab
GCSE qualifications		Some GCSEs grades D–G						●	●	
		1–3 GCSEs grades A–C and GCSEs grades D–F	●							
		4–5 GCSEs grades A–C and further training	●		●					
GCE Advanced-level qualifications		Any one academic A-level								
		Two or more academic A-levels		●		●	●			
		Chemistry, physics and/or maths	●							
		Chemistry and non-science subjects	●							
		Chemistry	●							
		Maths, physics and/or 2nd maths subject								
		Pure maths and non-science subject(s)								
		One maths subject								
		Physics								
		Physics and non-science subject(s)								
		Biology, chemistry and physics or maths	●							
		Biology, physics								
		Biology, chemistry	●							
		Biology and non-science subject(s)								
		Biology								
		Full-time post-A-level higher education course	A		E	E	E			
		Additional notes								

																			●	Saj	woodworking
																	(see Engineering)			Rav	Marine Engineer
																	(see Navy)				Marines
	A	●	●	●	●	●	●	●	●	●	●	●	●	●			●	●	●	Wad	Market gardener
	G														●	●				Ob	Market research
	A														●	●	●			Ob	Marketing
																	●	●	●	Ik	Massage
	A								●	●	●			●			●			Qog	Mathematician
																		●	●	Rax	Mechanic
																	(see Engineering)			Rax	Mechanical engineer
	A	●	●	●	●	●	●	●			●	●	●	●			●			Jax	Medical laboratory scientific officer
																●	●			Jog	Medical photographer
					●	●		●	●	●	●			●			●			Job	Medical physics technician
																	●	●		Cav	Medical records
																	●	●		Cat	Medical secretary
†3 A-levels usually required	E					●†								●†						Jab	Medicine
																					Merchant navy:
																	●			Yal	deck officer
																	●			Yal	engineering officer
																	●	●		Yal	radio officer
																			●	Yal	rating
	A			●	●	●	●	●	●	●	●	●	●	●			●			Qos	Metallurgist
																	●	●		Qos	Metallurgy technician
	A										●						●			Qol	Meteorologist
																			●	Rak/Ran	Meter reader
																	●			Jad	Midwife
																			●	Om	Milkroundsman/woman
																			●	Sab	Milk processing

		Millinery production	Miner	Mining engineer	Mine surveyor	Modeller + sculptor	Model – fashion
Note: A = available for this career; E = essential for this career; G = there is a graduate entry to this career although there are no directly relevant post-A-level courses	**Library Classification**	Sah	Rob	Rob	Um	Eb	Ot
GCSE qualifications	Some GCSEs grades D–G	●	●	(see Engineering)			●
	1–3 GCSEs grades A–C and GCSEs grades D–F	●	●	(see Engineering)			●
	4–5 GCSEs grades A–C and further training				●	●	
GCE Advanced-level qualifications	Any one academic A-level					●	
	Two or more academic A-levels					●	●
	Chemistry, physics and/or maths				●		
	Chemistry and non-science subjects				●		
	Chemistry				●		
	Maths, physics and/or 2nd maths subject				●		
	Pure maths and non-science subject(s)				●		
	One maths subject				●		
	Physics				●		
	Physics and non-science subject(s)				●		
	Biology, chemistry and physics or maths				●		
	Biology, physics				●		
	Biology, chemistry				●		
	Biology and non-science subject(s)				●		
	Biology				●		
	Full-time post-A-level higher education course				A	A	
	Additional notes						

164

Occupation	Code
Motor mechanic	Hae
Museum curator	Fag
Museum assistant	Fag
Museum conservator	Fag
Musician	Gad
Nature conservation: assistant regional officer	War
reserve warden	War
Naval architect	Rof
Navy: commissioned	Bab
non-commissioned	Bad
Nuclear engineer	Ran
Nursery nurse	Kec
Nurse	Jad
Nutritionist	Qon
Occupational therapist	Jar
Oil/gas drilling	Rob
Operational research	Paj
Ophthalmic optician	Jal
Ordnance survey	Ut
Organisation and methods	Pag
Orthoptics	Jam
Osteopath	Jod
Packer	S
Paint technologist	Sax
Paint and decorator	Uf
Panel beater	Ron

Naval architect (see Engineering)
Nuclear engineer (see Engineering)

G · G · E — †scientific A-levels help

G · A · A · E · E — †preferably science

E · A · E · E · A — †some preference for biology

165

		Park & garden maintenance	Patent examiner	Patent agent	Patrolman/woman – AA/RAC
	Note: A = available for this career E = essential for this career G = there is a graduate entry to this career although there are no directly relevant post-A-level courses				
	Library Classification	Wad	Rop	Rop	Rae
GCSE qualifications	Some GCSEs grades D–G	●			●
	1–3 GCSEs grades A–C and GCSEs grades D–F	●			●
	4–5 GCSEs grades A–C and further training	●			
GCE Advanced-level qualifications	Any one academic A-level				
	Two or more academic A-levels		●		
	Chemistry, physics and/or maths	●	●		
	Chemistry and non-science subjects	●	●		
	Chemistry	●		●†	
	Maths, physics and/or 2nd maths subject	●	●		
	Pure maths and non-science subject(s)	●	●		
	One maths subject	●	●	●†	
	Physics	●			
	Physics and non-science subject(s)	●			
	Biology, chemistry and physics or maths	●	●		
	Biology, physics	●			
	Biology, chemistry	●			
	Biology and non-science subject(s)	●			
	Biology	●			
	Full-time post-A-level higher education course	A	G	G	
Additional notes			†science degree		

Occupation	Code
Pensions consultant	Nan
Personnel management	Cas
Pharmacist	Jag
Photographer	Ev
Physicist	Qof
Physiological measurement technician	Job
Physiotherapist	Jan
Piano tuner	Soz
Pilot – aircraft	Yab
Pipe fitter	Uf
Plasterer	Uf
Plastics technologist	San
Plumber	Uf
Police	Mab
Post Office: administration	Cam
postal delivery	Yat
Pottery manufacture	Sad
Potter – design	Eg
Poultry husbandry	Wab
Printing: finisher and binder	Sar
machinery operator	Sar
technologist	Sar
Prison service: assistant governor	Mad
prison officer	Mad
Probation officer	Kem

†two science GCSEs required

†degree or diploma an advantage

		Production engineer	Professional sport	Psychologist	Public relations
	Note: A = available for this career E = essential for this career G = there is a graduate entry to this career although there are no directly relevant post-A-level courses				
	Library Classification	Rod	Gag	Kel	Og
GCSE qualifications	Some GCSEs grades D–G	(see Engineering)	●		
	1–3 GCSEs grades A–C and GCSEs grades D–F				
	4–5 GCSEs grades A–C and further training				●
GCE Advanced-level qualifications	Any one academic A-level				●
	Two or more academic A-levels			●	●
	Chemistry, physics and/or maths				
	Chemistry and non-science subjects				
	Chemistry				
	Maths, physics and/or 2nd maths subject				
	Pure maths and non-science subject(s)				
	One maths subject				
	Physics				
	Physics and non-science subject(s)				
	Biology, chemistry and physics or maths				
	Biology, physics				
	Biology, chemistry				
	Biology and non-science subject(s)				
	Biology				
	Full-time post-A-level higher education course			E	A
Additional notes					

168

Occupation	Code
Quarrying	Rob
Radio and TV servicing	Ral
Radiographer	Jap
Radio officer – merchant navy	Yal
Receptionist	Cav
Recreational management	Gaj
Refuse collection	Ij
Religion	Fam
Reporter	Fac
Residential social worker	Kec
Retail management	Of
Roofer	Uf
Royal Air Force	Bal (see Air Force)
Royal Marines	Bab (see Navy)
Royal Navy	Bab (see Navy)
Rubber technology	San
Sales representative	Om
Sawmiller	Saj
Science laboratory technician	Q
Sculptor	Eb
Secretary	Cat
Security work	Mag
Set design	Et
Sewing machinist	Sah

			Sheet metal worker	Shepherd/shepherdess	Shipbroker
Note: A = available for this career E = essential for this career G = there is a graduate entry to this career although there are no directly relevant post-A-level courses					
		Library Classification	Ron	Wab	Yas
GCSE qualifications		Some GCSEs grades D–G	●	●	
		1–3 GCSEs grades A–C and GCSEs grades D–F	●	●	●
		4–5 GCSEs grades A–C and further training		●	●
GCE Advanced-level qualifications		Any one academic A-level			●
		Two or more academic A-levels			●
		Chemistry, physics and/or maths			
		Chemistry and non-science subjects			
		Chemistry			
		Maths, physics and/or 2nd maths subject			
		Pure maths and non-science subject(s)			
		One maths subject			
		Physics			
		Physics and non-science subject(s)			
		Biology, chemistry and physics or maths			
		Biology, physics			
		Biology, chemistry			
		Biology and non-science subject(s)			
		Biology			
		Full-time post-A-level higher education course			
		Additional notes			

170

Occupation	Code		Notes
Signalman	Yaf		
Signwriter	Et		
Silversmith	Eg		A
Slater	Uf		E
Social worker	Keb		E
Solicitor	Lac		E
Speech therapist	Jas		
Sport	Gag		
Spray painter	Ron		
Stable worker	Wam		
Stage management	Gat		A
Statistician	Qog		A †
Stockbroker	Nal		G
Stock control	Of		
Stonemason	Uf		
Structural engineer	Un	(see Engineering)	E
Surgeon	Jab		A †
Surveyor	UP		A
Systems analyst	Pad		
Tailor	Sah		
Tanner	Saf		G
Tax inspector	Cab		E
Taxi driver	Yad		
Teacher	Fab		
Telephone engineer	Ral	(see Engineering)	
Telephonist	Cav		
Television producer	Gal		G
Television repair	Ral		

†maths A-level required

†3 A-levels usually required

171

Note:
A = available for this career
E = essential for this career
G = there is a graduate entry to this career although there are no directly relevant post-A-level courses

		Textile design (Ep)	Tiler (Uf)	Toolmaker (Rax)
	Library Classification	Ep	Uf	Rax
GCSE qualifications	Some GCSEs grades D–G		•	
	1–3 GCSEs grades A–C and GCSEs grades D–F		•	•
	4–5 GCSEs grades A–C and further training	•		
GCE Advanced-level qualifications	Any one academic A-level	•		
	Two or more academic A-levels	•		
	Chemistry, physics and/or maths			
	Chemistry and non-science subjects			
	Chemistry			
	Maths, physics and/or 2nd maths subject			
	Pure maths and non-science subject(s)			
	One maths subject			
	Physics			
	Physics and non-science subject(s)			
	Biology, chemistry and physics or maths			
	Biology, physics			
	Biology, chemistry			
	Biology and non-science subject(s)			
	Biology			
	Full-time post-A-level higher education course	A		

Additional notes

		Code													
administration			●			●					●	●			
Traffic warden	Maz			●											
Train driver	Yaf				●										
Translator	Fal					●	●	●	●	●					
Travel agent	Yap	†●													
Trawler fishing	Yam														
Typist	Cav														
Typographer	Sar														
Upholsterer	Saj														
Valuer	Um														
Ventilation engineer	Uj	(see Engineering)													
Veterinary nurse	Wal	●													

		Code													
Veterinary surgeon	Wal		●	●											
Waiter/waitress	Ic		●	●	●										
Wardrobe – films/TV/theatre	Gat		●												
Watch and clock repairer	Roz														
Weights and measures	Cop														
Welder	Ron														
Window cleaner	Ij		●		●	●	●								
Wine merchant	Of		●												
Woodworker	Saj														
Word processing	Cav		●	●		●									
Work study	Pag														
Writer	Fac		●	●		●									
Youth worker	Keg														
Zookeeper	Wam		●		●	●									
Zoologist	Qod		●		●	●									

† must include a language   A   A   A   E

†3 A-levels usually required   A   E

173

Where can you find out more?

Where can you find out more?

General

Which Subject? Which Career? by Alan Jamieson is a guide to choosing subjects at the key ages of 14, 16 and 18. It is available from Hobsons Publishing PLC, Bateman Street, Cambridge CB2 1LZ.

The Penguin Careers Guide, by Anna Alston (consultant editor Ruth Miller) is an excellent general careers book published by Penguin.

The Job Book, published for CRAC by Hobsons Publishing PLC, Bateman Street, Cambridge CB2 1LZ. This is the CRAC yearbook of education and training which gives details of opportunities offered by British employers to those entering employment, from school-leavers at 16 to post-graduates.

Your Choice of A-levels, by Mary Munro and Alan Jamieson. Published for CRAC by Hobsons Publishing PLC.

Decisions at 17/18+, by Michael Smith and Veronica Matthew. A sixth-formers' starting point for thought and discussion with parents, teachers and careers advisors on the range of choice after A-levels. Published for CRAC by Hobsons Publishing PLC.

Jobs and Careers after A-levels, by Mary Munro is for young people looking for a job rather than further study after A-levels. Published for CRAC by Hobsons Publishing PLC.

Working In Series, is the main series of careers booklets published by the Careers and Occupational Information Centre (COIC), Sales Department, Moorfoot, Sheffield S1 4PQ.

Courses

CRAC Degree Course Guides series. Thirty-six comparative first-degree course guides titled by degree subject; they are revised every two years, each half in alternate years. Published for CRAC by Hobsons Publishing PLC.

An excellent series of free leaflets about BTEC courses called Fact Sheets is obtainable from Publications Despatch Unit, Business and Technology Education Council, Central House, Upper Woburn Place, London WC1H 0HH.

Directory of Further Education, comprehensive guide to 65,000 further education courses leading to formal qualifications in the UK. Published for CRAC by Hobsons Publishing PLC.

The NATFHE Handbook of Initial Teacher Training, lists courses in education for prospective teachers. Published by the National Association of Teachers in Further and Higher Education and obtainable from Linneys ESL, Newgate Lane, Mansfield, Nottinghamshire NG18 2PA.

Polytechnic Courses Handbook, lists all the full-time and sandwich courses. Published by the Committee of Directors of Polytechnics, it is obtainable from Southport Book Distributors Ltd, 12–14 Slaidburn Crescent, Southport, Merseyside PR9 9YF.

A Compendium of Advanced Courses in Colleges of Further and Higher Education, is a comprehensive guide to advanced full-time and sandwich courses in polytechnics and other colleges outside the university sector, which is published by the Regional Advisory Councils in England and Wales. These Advisory Councils also publish comprehensive lists of all part-time, sandwich and full-time courses in their area:

East Anglian Regional Advisory Council for Further Education, 2 Looms Lane, Bury St Edmunds IP33 1HE.

East Midlands Further Education Council, Robins Wood House, Robins Wood Road, Aspley, Nottingham NG8 3NH.

London and South Eastern Regional Advisory Council for Further Education, 232 Vauxhall Bridge Road, London SW1V 1AU.

Northern Council for Further Education, 5 Grosvenor Villas, Grosvenor Road, Newcastle upon Tyne NE2 2RU.

North West Regional Association of Education Authorities, Town Hall, Walkden Road, Worsley, Manchester M28 4QE.

Southern Regional Council for Education and Training, 26 Bath Road, Reading RG1 6NT.

Association for Further Education and Training, Bishops Hull House, Bishops Hull, Taunton, Somerset TA1 5RA.

West Midlands Advisory Council for Further Education and Training, Mill Wharf, Mill Street, Birmingham B6 4BU.

Yorkshire and Humberside Association for Further and Higher Education, Bowling Green Terrace, Jack Lane, Leeds LS11 9SX.

Welsh Joint Education Committee, 245 Western Avenue, Llandaff, Cardiff CF5 2YX.

University Entrance: The Official Guide. Association of Commonwealth Universities for the Committee of Vice-Chancellors and Principals. Obtainable from Sheed and Ward, 14 Coopers Row, London EC3N 2BH.

Acknowledgements

The authors would like to acknowledge with grateful thanks the assistance of the following:

Peter Andrews, sometime Chairman, Standing Committee of the CSE Examination Boards

Catherine Avent, formerly Senior Inspector Careers Guidance, ILEA

Rt Hon Kenneth Baker, formerly of the Information Technology Division, Department of Industry

Helen Ehrenstein, Committee of Vice-Chancellors and Principals of the Universities of the United Kingdom

R E J Elliott, Unigate Foods, Yeovil

John C Fogg, Press and Public Relations Officer, British Rail

Ann Gathercole, Head of Biology, Filton High School, Bristol

G Hobbs, Director, YMCA Special Programmes

J McKelvey, Information Branch, Manpower Services Commission

J Scarborough, Director, International Electronics

Alan West, Youth Cohort Study (England and Wales), 1985, Manpower Services Commission

Roger Williams, Press Officer, Manpower Services Commission

The Business and Technician Education Council

The Engineering Careers Information Service

Marconi Electronic Devices Ltd

The Information Centre of the School Curriculum Development Committee

The Publicity Department of the CPVE

The Leicestershire Careers Service Information Unit, City Careers Centre, Pocklingtons Walk, Leicester

The CBI for extracts from *Towards a Skills Revolution* (1989).

Kate Phillips, Greater Peterborough TEC

Decisions at 17/18+

Authors: Michael Smith and Veronica Matthew
Ages: 16 – 18

Designed with the school and college leaver in mind, **Decisions at 17/18+** helps students to plan the next stage after A-levels by examining all the options that are available. It attempts to weigh up the options available after the sixth form and to show where the chosen subjects might lead.

Each course of action can have its own special attractions and discovering the best route means considering personality, academic record, financial resources and local employment opportunities.

This book will help students accurately to assess their own potential and so make the right decisions.

198×126mm, 208pp, paperback.

Available from Hobsons Publishing PLC, Bateman Street, Cambridge CB2 1LZ.

Jobs and Careers after A-levels

Author: Mary Munro
Ages: 16 – 18

An invaluable guide for sixth-formers to the many opportunities available and jobs to be found at this stage. This book will help young people to find out about them and to know where to look and who to ask.

Career profiles of 43 successful jobseekers help to put the general advice into perspective and show the reality of starting a job after A-levels.

198×126mm, 232pp, paperback.

Available from Hobsons Publishing PLC, Bateman Street, Cambridge CB2 1LZ.